ANNE WILLAN'S
LOOK & COOK

Meat Classics

ANNE WILLAN'S
LOOK & COOK

Meat Classics

A DORLING KINDERSLEY BOOK

Created and Produced by
CARROLL & BROWN LIMITED
5 Lonsdale Road
London NW6 6RA

Editorial Director Jeni Wright
Editors Norma MacMillan
Stella Vayne
Sally Poole
Art Editor Vicky Zentner
Designers Lucy De Rosa
Lyndel Donaldson
Wendy Rogers
Mary Staples
Lisa Webb

First published in Canada in 1992 by
Stoddart Publishing Co. Limited
34 Lesmill Road
Toronto, Canada
M3B 2T6

Canadian Cataloguing in Publication Data

Willan, Anne
Meat classics

(Anne Willan's Look & cook)
ISBN 0-7737-2631-4

1. Cookery (Meat). I. Title. II. Series: Willan,
Anne. Anne Willan's Look & cook.

TX749.W5 1993   641.6'6   C92-093953-8

Reproduced by Colourscan, Singapore
Printed and bound in Italy by A. Mondadori, Verona

CONTENTS

MEAT

THE LOOK & COOK APPROACH

Welcome to **Meat Classics,** and the *Look & Cook* series. These volumes are designed to be the simplest, most informative cookbooks you'll ever own. They are the closest I can come to sharing my techniques for cooking my own favorite recipes without actually being with you in the kitchen looking over your shoulder.

EQUIPMENT

Equipment and ingredients often determine whether or not you can cook a particular dish, so *Look & Cook* illustrates everything you need at the beginning of each recipe. You'll see at a glance how long a recipe takes to cook, how many servings it makes, what the finished dish looks like, and how much preparation can be done ahead. When you start to cook, you'll find the preparation and cooking are organized into easy-to-follow steps. Each stage is color-coded and everything is shown in photographs with brief text to go with each step. You will never be in doubt about what it is you are doing, why you are doing it, or how it should look.

INGREDIENTS

🍽 SERVES 4   🥣 WORK TIME 15-20 MINUTES   🍲 COOKING TIME 20-25 MINUTES

I've also included helpful hints and ideas under "Anne Says." These may list an alternative ingredient or piece of equipment, or sometimes the reason for using a certain method is explained, or there is some advice on mastering a particular technique. Similarly, if there is a crucial stage in a recipe when things can go wrong, I've included some warnings called "Take Care."

Many of the photographs are annotated to pinpoint why certain pieces of equipment work best, or how the food should look at that stage of cooking. Because presentation is so important, a picture of the finished dish and serving suggestions are at the end of each recipe.

Thanks to all this information, you can't go wrong. I'll be with you every step of the way. So please, come with me into the kitchen to look, cook, and create some delicious **Meat Classics.**

WHY MEAT?

*Nutritious and full of flavor, meat has long been a centerpiece
for festive and family menus. Meat adapts to the many different styles of
cooking that are found worldwide, though individual cuts may vary
from country to country and even region to region. The great variety
of beef, veal, lamb, and pork offers a choice to please every taste.*

RECIPE CHOICE

The different cuts and types of meat available offer an almost
limitless number of dishes. You'll find here an international
assortment, from American Southwestern Barbecued Pork
and British Steak and Wild Mushroom
Pie to Japanese Pork and Ginger
Sukiyaki, with an array of
traditional and contemporary
techniques and ingredients
to match. I've divided
the book into two
sections, for quick
and slow cooking.
Quickly cooked
meat dishes
require less
than an
hour, so
they are
perfect for a
busy week night. For
example, Russian Beef Sauté
can be ready in 35 minutes. More slowly cooked meat dishes
include stews that simmer gently in the oven, such as
Provençal Beef Stew, and roasts such as Roast Leg of Lamb
with White Beans.

QUICK COOKING

Turkish Ground Lamb Kebabs: Lamb and herb mixture is
shaped into cylinders and cooked on skewers to serve
with a cool cucumber and yogurt sauce. *Indian
Ground Lamb Kebabs:* Spicy kebabs are served
with cucumber salad. *Southwestern Barbecued
Pork with Salsa:* Pork loin, marinated in
pungent barbecue sauce, is grilled to serve
with crisp tortilla strips and salsa. *Barbecued
Steak:* Beef steak, basted with barbecue sauce
while grilling, has salsa accompaniment.
Russian Beef Sauté: Tender beef strips and
mushrooms have a tangy sour cream and mustard
sauce. *Beef Sauté with Paprika:* Strips of red bell pepper
and paprika add color to the beef. *Veal Scaloppine with
Sage and Prosciutto:* Flattened veal scaloppine, topped
with prosciutto and
fresh sage leaves,
are sautéed in
butter. *Veal Piccate
with Mushrooms
and Marsala:* Small
scaloppine are served
in a rich sauce. *Pork and
Ginger Sukiyaki:* Pork slices
are perfumed with ginger, then
cooked sukiyaki-style with mushrooms and scallions in soy
sauce and sake wine. *Beef, Ginger, and Sesame Sukiyaki:*
Sesame oil and a sprinkling of sesame seeds add nutty
flavor and fragrance to traditional beef sukiyaki. *Rack of
Lamb with Sautéed Cucumbers and Mint:* The classic duo
of roast lamb with mint is joined by sautéed cucumbers.
Rack of Lamb Coated with Parsley and Breadcrumbs: A
crispy coating of parsley and buttered breadcrumbs covers
succulent rack of lamb. *Minute Steak Marchand de Vin:*
Delicate steaks cut from the tenderloin are pan-fried and
served with a simple sauce of red wine and shallots. *Minute
Steak Dijonnaise:* Tangy Dijon-style mustard and cream
flavor the golden sauce for minute steaks. *Butterflied Leg of
Lamb:* Boned leg of lamb is laid flat and marinated in garlic
and herbs, then broiled. *Butterflied Loin of Pork:* Garlic,
herbs, and mustard infuse boneless pork loin, opened flat
for broiling. *Lamb Chops in Paper Cases with Fennel:*
Browned loin chops on a bed of fennel and tomatoes bake
gently in a parchment paper case. *Lamb Chops in Paper
Cases with Leeks:* Sautéed leeks, tomatoes, and herbs
complement lamb chops baked in paper.

SLOW COOKING

Tenderloin of Beef Stuffed with Mushrooms: For a grand occasion, a whole tenderloin is stuffed with a "duxelles" mixture of chopped mushrooms, parsley, garlic, and bacon, and served with a Madeira sauce. *Tournedos of Beef with Mushrooms:* Thick tenderloin steaks, spread with mushroom "duxelles," are served on rounds of turnip and topped with Madeira sauce. *Roast Leg of Lamb with White Beans:* Garlic-studded leg of lamb is served Brittany-style with white beans and baked tomatoes. *Lemon Roast Leg of Lamb with Zucchini Gratins:* Slivers of lemon zest and garlic spike the lamb, which is served with baked zucchini and Gruyère gratins. *Italian Braised Veal Shanks:* The classic Milanese "osso buco" is topped with a zesty "gremolata" of parsley, lemon zest, and garlic. *Braised Lamb Shanks:* Tomato, garlic, and fresh rosemary top lamb shanks braised in a red wine sauce. *Aunt Sally's Meat Loaf:* Here the American favorite is made with ground beef and veal, bacon, spinach, and fresh herbs, spiced with Worcestershire sauce. *Pork Loaf with Apricots:* This sweet and savory variation adds a layer of dried apricots to a pork-based meat loaf. *Baked Fresh Ham with Orange:* Fresh pork ham is baked slowly, basted with fresh orange juice, then glazed and topped with orange slices and cloves, and served with a spiced Grand Marnier sauce. *Fresh Ham Baked in Cider:* Apple cider bastes the ham, which is served with baked apples stuffed with brown sugar and raisins. *Indian Braised Lamb:* Cubes of lamb are gently cooked in spiced yogurt and cream in this fragrant dish. *Moroccan Spiced Lamb:* A change of spice and a toasted almond topping give lamb Moroccan flavors. *Roast Rib of Beef Pebronata:* Juicy beef rib roast is served with a brilliant red tomato and bell pepper sauce from Corsica. *Roast Rib of Beef with Yorkshire Pudding:* The classic British Sunday lunch of tender beef and golden batter puddings is served with a rich gravy. *Roast Rib of Beef with Glazed Baby Onions, Turnips, and Carrots:* Vegetables glazed with butter and sugar make a winter garnish for rib of beef. *Provençal Beef Stew:* Country "daube" simmers beef in red wine with bacon, salt pork, herbs, garlic, distinctive

black olives, and zest of orange. *Provençal Lamb Stew with Green Olives:* Here cubes of lamb replace beef, with green olives instead of black. *Chili con Carne:* Texas-style chili is made with tender beef, tomatoes, and lots of spice. *Mexican Chili con Carne:* Chili goes south of the border, with the addition of unsweetened chocolate, plus cinnamon and cloves. *Burgundy Pot Roast:* Classic Burgundian garnish of bacon, baby onions, and mushrooms is perfect with beef pot roasted in red wine. *Flemish Pot Roast with Dark Beer:* Beer, carrots, and lots of onions give good flavor to beef pot roast. *French Hot Pot (Pot-au-Feu):* French country favorite presents beef simmered with aromatic vegetables to spoon-cutting tenderness and a separate course of rich broth. *Potée:* Pork shoulder is cooked with smoked bacon and cabbage wedges. *Pork Noisettes with Cornbread and Cranberries:* Thick pork noisettes with a cornbread, pecan, and celery stuffing are accompanied by a tart cranberry and wine sauce. *Pork Noisettes with Cornbread and Apple Rings:* Stuffed noisettes are served with a creamy sauce and caramelized apple rings. *Steak and Wild Mushroom Pie:* Cubes of steak cooked with meaty wild mushrooms are topped with a quick puff-pastry crust. *Individual Victorian Steak and Kidney Pies:* Kidneys and oysters are added to the steak filling in these individual pies. *Hungarian Beef Goulash:* Hearty beef and bell pepper stew, highly flavored with paprika and caraway seeds, has tiny dumplings. *Hungarian Veal Goulash:* Chunks of veal, potatoes, and green bell peppers are cooked in a pungent paprika, garlic, and tomato sauce.

EQUIPMENT

Meat cuts and techniques vary widely, but the list of specialized equipment needed to execute them is short. You'll need a chef's knife for trimming and cutting meat into pieces, whether cubes or slices. For boning, use a boning knife; the sharp tip of the blade allows you to maneuver around the bone without losing too much flesh and the handle is shaped for a firm grip. All knives should be sharpened on a steel each time you use them. For carving, a knife with a flexible blade is helpful, long or short depending on the cut.

Stews and slow-cooked meat dishes demand an assortment of casseroles and pans with lids. Roasting pans in medium and large sizes are required for browning and roasting, and a sauté pan or large frying pan is needed for sautés. An oval pie dish is classic for the steak pie, and you'll need parchment paper for lamb chops in paper cases and metal skewers for lamb kebabs. A meat thermometer comes in handy for testing the temperature of cooked meat, but a metal skewer also works well. Use an electric or hand meat grinder for grinding beef, lamb, or pork, with a food processor as an alternative; or save time and have the butcher do the work. Cooking meat on a barbecue grill adds smoky flavor, but your broiler is quite acceptable as a substitute.

INGREDIENTS

Meat often stands alone as a roast, or broiled chop or steak. The many ingredients that act as partners tend to bring out the full flavor of the meat itself.

Fresh herbs like parsley, thyme, coriander (cilantro), oregano and sage nicely complement all meat, whether in stews or roasted. The classic herb partners for lamb are rosemary and mint. A wide variety of spices, such as cayenne, cinnamon, coriander seed, cloves, caraway seeds, chili powder, ginger, mace, nutmeg, cumin, paprika, cardamom, and turmeric add depth and often international flavor. The allium family – onion, garlic, and shallot – is essential to many dishes, while olives and piquant aromatics, such as hot chili peppers and fresh ginger root, add distinctive taste to others. Mustard provides good balance in various sauces as well as a coating for ham.

"Meat and vegetables" has become a catchphrase, whether you think of carrots, celery, leeks, or tomatoes to flavor a sauce, or mushrooms, fennel, bell peppers, or cucumbers as the finishing touch. Fruit, from apples and oranges to apricots and cranberries, are a tasty, juicy addition to meat dishes, particularly succulent pork. Even sumptuous chocolate (unsweetened) appears in a sauce for beef, while molasses adds sweetness

to barbecued pork and brown sugar coats baked fresh ham. Crumbly cornbread does double duty as a stuffing for pork noisettes and the accompaniment to chili.

The flavor of meat is often intensified by the addition of beef or veal stock. Wine, whether red or white, is a natural partner for meat, while Madeira, pastis, sake, mirin, and Grand Marnier blend well and add a lift of flavor to savory sauces and glazes. Beer and cider appear in many regional meat dishes. Milk products, such as sour cream and heavy cream, add richness and smooth taste to sauces for many meats; yogurt acts as the cooking liquid and tenderizer in Indian Braised Lamb.

TECHNIQUES

The different meats in these recipes call for an assortment of useful techniques. You will learn how to trim large cuts of excess fat and sinew before cooking, and about cutting meat into large cubes for stew or smaller pieces for chili – the size must be uniform to ensure even cooking. You will see how to carve neat minute steaks and the thin slices needed for pork sukiyaki, how to grind meat, and how to pound scaloppine or medallions to very thin slices for quicker cooking. A few more advanced methods of preparing meat include preparing elegant rack of lamb and butterflying a lamb leg by removing the bones and cutting so it will lie flat.

Cooking methods for meat are diverse; even the style for a simple stew can differ. For some, cubes of meat are first browned to lock in juices before simmering in flavored liquid; in others, the meat pieces are added raw and cooked long and gently to tenderize them and produce a rich sauce. Large pieces of meat may be simmered whole in plenty of liquid or they may be pot-roasted by cooking them in their own juices with a small amount of stock until very tender. Tender cuts are usually roasted; you will learn the method of searing them in a very hot oven to form a browned crust, then reducing the temperature to cook the meat thoroughly. You will also learn to test the internal temperature of meat using a skewer or a meat thermometer.

For quickly cooked meats, the popular methods of pan-frying and broiling are explained. From small strips of beef to veal scaloppine and beef steaks, pan-frying is simple and fast, preserving flavor and tenderness. Broiling quickly cooks a variety of meats from beef steaks to butterflied leg of lamb, first marinating them to ensure juiciness. A more unusual technique is used for lamb chops in paper cases. Here the cooking must be carefully timed so the lamb is perfectly done in its parchment container.

TURKISH GROUND LAMB KEBABS

Sis Köfte

🍽 SERVES 6   🥣 WORK TIME 30-35 MINUTES   ♨ COOKING TIME 10-15 MINUTES

EQUIPMENT

chef's knife

small knife   pastry brush

wooden spoon

large metal spoon

metal spatula

6 metal skewers

colander   food processor*

small frying pan

bowls

chopping board

grater

*meat grinder can also be used

Lamb is the traditional Mediterranean meat, and each country from Morocco to Greece has its own specialties. In Turkey, ground lamb is mixed with onion, garlic, and cumin, formed into cylinders around skewers as kebabs, and broiled.

GETTING AHEAD

The ground meat mixture and yogurt sauce can be made up to 8 hours ahead and kept covered in the refrigerator; the flavors will mellow. The kebabs are best cooked just before serving.

SHOPPING LIST

2 lb	boneless lamb shoulder
1	large onion
3	garlic cloves
3-5	sprigs of fresh mint
3-5	sprigs of parsley
2 tsp	ground cumin
	salt and pepper
	olive oil, for brushing
	For the yogurt sauce
1	large cucumber
1 tsp	salt
1	garlic clove
2 cups	plain yogurt

INGREDIENTS

boneless lamb shoulder

cucumber

plain yogurt   onion

parsley   olive oil

ground cumin   garlic cloves

fresh mint

ORDER OF WORK

1 MAKE THE YOGURT SAUCE

2 PREPARE THE GROUND MEAT MIXTURE

3 PREPARE AND COOK THE KEBABS

1 MAKE THE YOGURT SAUCE

1 Wipe and trim the cucumber. Grate the cucumber, with the skin, into a large bowl. Stir in the salt well, so that it is evenly distributed.

Press cucumber firmly against large holes as you grate into big bowl

Green skin adds color to grated cucumber

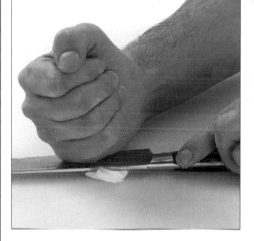

2 Set the colander over a bowl. Transfer the grated cucumber to the colander and let drain 10 minutes to draw out excess moisture.

3 Set the flat side of the chef's knife on top of the garlic clove and strike it with your fist. Discard the skin and finely chop the garlic.

4 Put the yogurt in a large bowl. Remove more water from the cucumber by squeezing it in your fist. Add the cucumber to the yogurt. Stir in the garlic with salt to taste. Cover and chill.

2 PREPARE THE GROUND MEAT MIXTURE

1 Trim any fat and sinew from the lamb. Cut the meat into small chunks. Peel and trim the onion and cut it into chunks.

2 Work the chunks of lamb and onion in the food processor, in batches if necessary, until smooth, 1-2 minutes. Put the lamb and onion into a large bowl.

ANNE SAYS
"Do not overwork the lamb in the processor, or the kebabs will be tough."

To adjust seasoning, fry small piece of mixture and taste

3 Set the flat side of the chef's knife on top of each garlic clove and strike it with your fist. Discard the skin and finely chop the garlic. Strip the mint and parsley leaves from the stems, reserving 6 mint leaves for garnish, and pile them on the chopping board. Finely chop the leaves.

4 Add the cumin, salt, pepper, garlic, and herbs to the meat. Beat with the wooden spoon until all the ingredients are thoroughly combined, 1-2 minutes.

5 To test the mixture for seasoning, fry a spoonful of the meat mixture in the small frying pan until browned on both sides. Taste and add more salt and pepper to the uncooked mixture if necessary.

3 PREPARE AND COOK THE KEBABS

1 Heat the broiler and set the rack 2 inches from the heat. Wet your hands and roll one-third of the mixture into a cylinder 1 inch in diameter. Repeat to make 2 more cylinders. Cut each one into 6 equal lengths.

Meat is easy to shape and will not stick to your hands if they are damp

2 Brush the skewers and broiler rack with olive oil. Thread the meat onto the skewers, pressing the cylinders well into shape; put the kebabs on the broiler rack.

3 With the pastry brush, brush the kebabs with olive oil, and broil them until they are brown on top and sputtering, 5-7 minutes.

Be sure to brown meat on all sides

4 Turn the skewers and continue cooking until browned on the other side, 5-7 minutes longer. The meat should be well done but still juicy in the center.

🍴 **TO SERVE**

Serve the kebabs on a bed of tabouleh salad, garnished with the reserved mint leaves, and decorated with tomatoes and black olives, if you like. Pass the yogurt sauce separately.

Kebabs are served sizzling on tabouleh salad

Cool yogurt sauce complements kebabs

INDIAN GROUND LAMB KEBABS

Additional spices and fresh coriander help transform these kebabs into an Indian feast.

1 In place of the yogurt sauce, make a cucumber and yogurt salad: Peel and trim 2 large cucumbers, cut them in half, and scoop out the seeds with a teaspoon. Slice the cucumbers, omitting the salting and draining. Mix the cucumber with 1 cup plain yogurt, the finely chopped garlic, and salt to taste. Chill until serving.

2 Trim and grind the lamb and onion as directed. Finely chop the garlic. In place of the mint, chop the leaves from 3-5 sprigs of fresh coriander (cilantro) with the parsley.

3 Mix the ground meat and onion with the garlic, herbs, and cumin, adding 1½ tsp ground ginger, 2 tsp ground turmeric, 2 tsp ground coriander, and ½ tsp ground cloves. Shape the mixture into 1-inch ovals, skewer, and cook as directed, 3-5 minutes per side.

4 Remove the kebabs from the skewers, if you like, and serve with the cucumber salad on a bed of saffron rice. Garnish with fresh coriander leaves.

13

SOUTHWESTERN BARBECUED PORK WITH SALSA

🍽 SERVES 6　　WORK TIME 35-40 MINUTES*　　BAKING TIME 40-50 MINUTES

EQUIPMENT

rubber gloves

waxed paper

pastry brush

paper towels

chef's knife

citrus juicer

bowls

meat cleaver**

large metal spoon

small knife

slotted spoon

tongs

sauté pan

food processor***

plate

shallow dish

frying pan

rubber spatula

** heavy-based pan or rolling pin can also be used

*** blender can also be used

Here pork loin is sliced and flattened, then marinated in a pungent barbecue sauce, and grilled to serve with a fresh salsa made with coriander and jalapeño peppers. Slices of avocado and crisp tortilla strips complete the dish.

plus 2-8 hours marinating time

SHOPPING LIST

2 lb	boned pork loin
3	ripe avocados
1	lemon
3	corn tortillas
1/3 cup	vegetable oil, more if needed
	For the salsa and barbecue sauce
2	large onions
4	garlic cloves
3-4	sprigs of fresh coriander (cilantro)
2	fresh jalapeño peppers
2 1/2 lb	tomatoes
1	yellow or red bell pepper
1	lemon
	Tabasco sauce
	salt
1 tbsp	coriander seeds
4	limes
1/4 cup	red wine vinegar
1/2 cup	molasses
3 tbsp	vegetable oil

INGREDIENTS

boned pork loin

avocados

molasses

corn tortillas

fresh jalapeño peppers

limes

onions

yellow bell pepper

red wine vinegar

vegetable oil

garlic cloves

coriander seeds

tomatoes

fresh coriander

lemon

Tabasco sauce

ORDER OF WORK

1 MAKE THE SALSA AND BARBECUE SAUCE

2 PREPARE THE PORK LOIN

3 PREPARE THE GARNISH AND GRILL THE PORK

1 MAKE THE SALSA AND BARBECUE SAUCE

Coriander is delicate so chop coarsely to avoid bruising

1 Peel the onions, leaving a little of the root attached, and cut in half. Slice each half horizontally toward the root, leaving the slices attached at the root end, then slice vertically, again leaving the root end uncut. Cut across to make dice.

2 Set the flat side of the chef's knife on top of each garlic clove and strike it with your fist. Discard the skin and finely chop the garlic.

3 Strip the coriander leaves from the stems, pile them on the chopping board, then finely chop the leaves. Core, seed, and dice the jalapeño peppers (see box, below).

HOW TO CORE, SEED, AND DICE FRESH HOT CHILI PEPPERS

Fresh hot chili peppers, such as jalapeños, must be finely chopped so their heat is spread evenly through the dish. For a hotter flavor you can add the seeds, too. Be sure to wear rubber gloves, and to avoid contact with eyes, because the hot chili peppers can burn your hands and eyes.

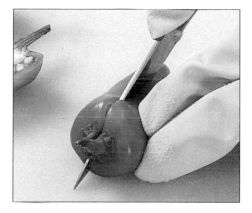

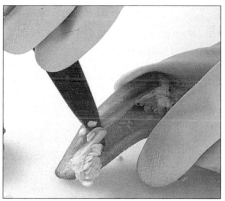

1 Cut the peppers lengthwise in half with a small knife.

2 Cut out the core and fleshy white "ribs" and scrape out the seeds.

3 Set each half cut-side up and thinly slice it lengthwise.

Slice very thinly so dice will be fine

4 Hold the strips together and cut across into very fine dice.

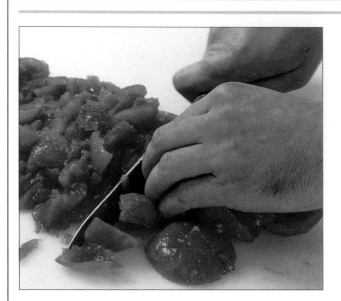

Contrasting textures
are essence of
salsa

Mingled cool and
fiery flavors will
stimulate tastebuds

4 Cut the cores from the tomatoes and score an "x" on the base of each with the tip of the small knife. Immerse in boiling water until the skin starts to split, 8-15 seconds. Transfer at once to a bowl of cold water. When cold, peel off the skin. Cut the tomatoes crosswise in half and squeeze out the seeds. Chop each half.

ANNE SAYS
"*A portion of these ingredients will be used for the salsa, the rest for the barbecue sauce.*"

5 To make the salsa, combine half of the onion, one-quarter of the garlic, the coriander, half of the jalapeño peppers, and one-third of the tomatoes in a large bowl.

Yellow bell pepper
adds color and
crunchiness
to salsa

6 With a sharp movement, twist the core out of the bell pepper, then halve it, and scrape out the seeds. Cut away the white ribs on the inside. Set each half cut-side down on the work surface, flatten it with the heel of your hand, and slice lengthwise into strips. Gather the strips together in a pile and cut across into dice.

7 Add the diced pepper to the salsa ingredients. Squeeze the lemon and pour the juice into the salsa. Season to taste with Tabasco sauce and salt, then cover and refrigerate.

Freshly squeezed lime juice is delightfully aromatic

Coriander seeds introduce fragrant accent

8 To make the barbecue sauce, heat the oil in the sauté pan, add the remaining onion, garlic, and jalapeño peppers, and sauté, stirring, until soft but not browned, 3-4 minutes. Add the coriander seeds and the remaining tomatoes. Squeeze the limes and pour the juice into the sauce.

9 Cook over medium heat, stirring occasionally, until reduced and thickened, about 15 minutes.

10 Add the red wine vinegar, bring to a boil, and reduce until thickened again, 8-10 minutes.

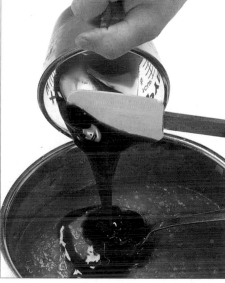

11 Stir in the molasses and simmer the mixture 1-2 minutes longer. Season with salt.

12 Let the sauce cool slightly, then purée it in the food processor and let cool completely.

2 PREPARE THE PORK LOIN

1 Trim fat and any sinew from the pork loin and cut the meat across into 6 even slices. Put a slice between 2 sheets of waxed paper and flatten to a thickness of about ¹/₂ inch with the flat side of the meat cleaver. Put each remaining slice between waxed paper and flatten in the same way.

ANNE SAYS
"Flattening the meat ensures that it will cook quickly and evenly and not dry out."

Cut equal slices so pork cooks evenly

There is no need to trim off every thin sliver of fat

2 Put the pork slices into the shallow dish, cover with the cold barbecue sauce, and turn the meat so that it is thoroughly coated with the sauce. Cover the dish and refrigerate at least 2 hours and up to 8 hours.

3 PREPARE THE GARNISH AND GRILL THE PORK

1 Heat the broiler or a charcoal grill. Halve each avocado. With a chopping movement, imbed the blade of the chef's knife in each avocado pit and, twisting gently, lift it free. Or, scoop out the pits with a spoon.

2 Squeeze the lemon. With the small knife, peel the skin from each avocado half. Cut the halves crosswise into thin slices and lay them on the plate. Brush immediately with the lemon juice.

3 Stack the tortillas and cut them into ¹/₄-inch strips. Heat the oil in the frying pan, add the tortilla strips, and fry over high heat, turning once, until crisp, 1-2 minutes. Transfer to paper towels and keep warm in a low oven.

4 Brush the broiler rack with oil. Take each slice of pork from the barbecue sauce with the tongs, allowing excess sauce to drip off, and put on the broiler rack. Cook about 2 inches from the heat until brown and slightly charred, 5-7 minutes.

Oiled rack keeps pork from sticking

5 Turn the meat slices over, brush each one with barbecue sauce, and cook until well browned and no longer pink inside, about 5-7 minutes.

ANNE SAYS
"The meat should feel firm when you press it with a finger."

🍽 **TO SERVE**
Transfer the grilled pork to warmed individual plates. Spoon some salsa onto a few salad leaves, if you like, and top with an herb sprig. Add the tortilla strips and avocado slices.

Avocado slices are cool contrast with spicy pork

VARIATION

BARBECUED STEAK

Here T-bone or strip steaks replace the pork for an equally delicious result.

1 Prepare the salsa and barbecue sauce as directed.
2 Trim 6 T-bone or strip steaks of fat and any sinew; they should be about $3/4$ inch thick. Marinate the steaks in the barbecue sauce as directed. Omit the avocados and tortillas.
3 Heat the broiler or charcoal grill, and grill the steaks as directed, allowing 3-4 minutes for rare meat or 5-6 minutes for medium-done meat. Brush the tops of the steaks with more sauce as they cook. Turn the meat over, brush with more barbecue sauce, and cook 3-4 minutes for rare, 5-6 minutes for medium. When rare, the steak will feel spongy when pressed with a finger and medium meat will resist slightly when pressed.
4 Take the steaks from the heat and brush with a little more sauce. Serve with the salsa on a bed of fresh young spinach leaves and herb sprigs.

— **GETTING AHEAD** —
The salsa and barbecue sauce can be made 2-3 days in advance and kept, covered, in the refrigerator. The meat can be prepared and marinated up to 8 hours ahead, then grilled just before serving.

RUSSIAN BEEF SAUTE

EQUIPMENT

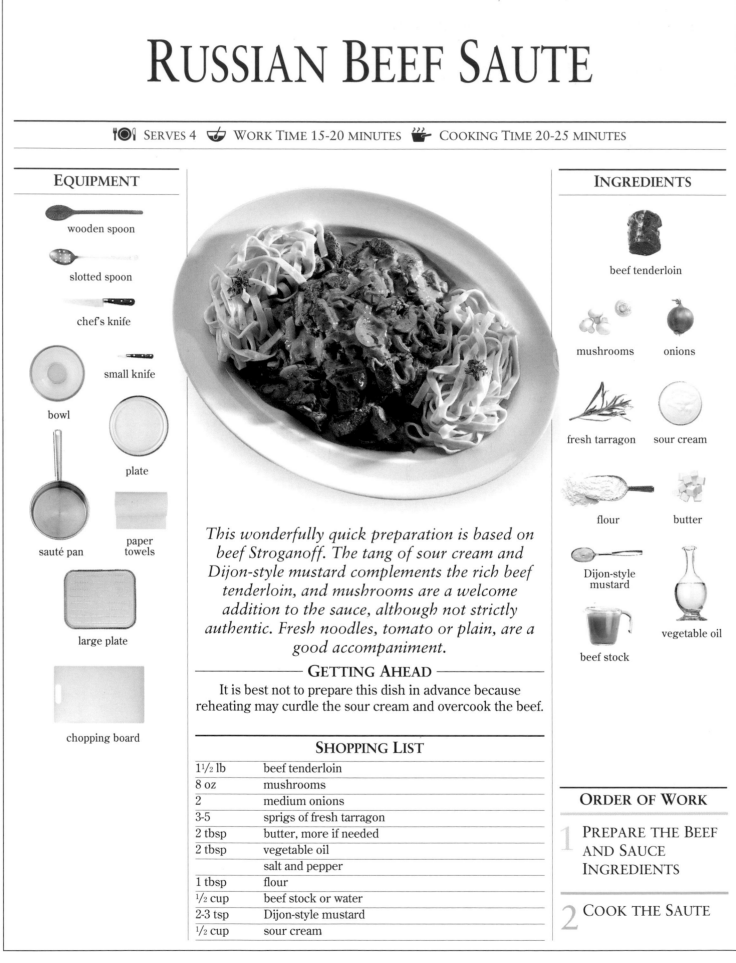

wooden spoon

slotted spoon

chef's knife

small knife

bowl

plate

sauté pan

paper towels

large plate

chopping board

INGREDIENTS

beef tenderloin

mushrooms

onions

fresh tarragon

sour cream

flour

butter

Dijon-style mustard

vegetable oil

beef stock

This wonderfully quick preparation is based on beef Stroganoff. The tang of sour cream and Dijon-style mustard complements the rich beef tenderloin, and mushrooms are a welcome addition to the sauce, although not strictly authentic. Fresh noodles, tomato or plain, are a good accompaniment.

GETTING AHEAD

It is best not to prepare this dish in advance because reheating may curdle the sour cream and overcook the beef.

SHOPPING LIST

1½ lb	beef tenderloin
8 oz	mushrooms
2	medium onions
3-5	sprigs of fresh tarragon
2 tbsp	butter, more if needed
2 tbsp	vegetable oil
	salt and pepper
1 tbsp	flour
½ cup	beef stock or water
2-3 tsp	Dijon-style mustard
½ cup	sour cream

ORDER OF WORK

1 PREPARE THE BEEF AND SAUCE INGREDIENTS

2 COOK THE SAUTE

1 PREPARE THE BEEF AND SAUCE INGREDIENTS

1 Trim the tenderloin of any fat or sinew. Cut the meat into 1/2-inch slices. Cut each slice into 1/2-inch strips about 3 inches long.

Cut strips of equal size so they cook evenly

2 Wipe the mushroom caps with damp paper towels and trim the stems even with the caps. Set the mushrooms stem-side down on the chopping board and slice them.

3 Peel the onions and cut a thin slice from one side of each so that the onion sits flat on the chopping board. Cut the onions into slices of medium thickness. Strip the tarragon leaves from the stems and chop the leaves.

2 COOK THE SAUTE

Juice is sealed in as meat strips brown over high heat

1 Heat half of the butter and oil in the sauté pan until starting to brown. Add half of the beef strips, sprinkle with a little salt and pepper, and cook over very high heat, stirring, until the meat is well browned but still rare in the center, 2-3 minutes. Remove the meat with the slotted spoon and add more butter if the pan is dry. Brown the remaining beef in the same way, then remove it and set aside.

Stir in flour until
it is absorbed by
mushrooms

2 Heat the remaining butter and oil
in the sauté pan, add the onions,
separating the slices into rings, and
sauté over medium heat until softened
and browned, stirring occasionally,
5-7 minutes. Transfer them to a bowl
with the slotted spoon.

3 Add the mushrooms
to the pan and sauté
until all the moisture has
evaporated, 4-5 minutes.
Stirring constantly, add the
flour and cook 1 minute.

4 Pour in the stock and bring
to a boil, stirring so the
sauce thickens smoothly.

Stock combines
with flour to
make rich sauce

5 Return the onions to the pan, add
salt and pepper, and simmer
2 minutes. Stir in the mustard and
heat gently without boiling.

! TAKE CARE !
*If the mustard boils, the sauce will
be bitter.*

6 Return the beef and its juices to the sauté pan and heat gently but thoroughly, 2-3 minutes. If the beef is overcooked, it will be tough.

Tangy sour cream is favorite Russian flavoring

7 Stir in the sour cream and heat the sauté about 1 minute longer. Taste for seasoning.

ANNE SAYS
"Do not let the mixture get too hot or the sour cream may curdle."

🍴 TO SERVE
Serve immediately with cooked fresh noodles. Sprinkle with the chopped tarragon.

Fresh noodles are an excellent accompaniment

Beef strips are lightly sautéed so they are still rare in center

V A R I A T I O N

BEEF SAUTE WITH PAPRIKA

Here paprika is added with red bell peppers for a colorful version of Russian Beef Sauté.

1 Trim and cut the beef tenderloin as directed in the main recipe.
2 Prepare the onions as directed; omit the mushrooms and the mustard.
3 With a sharp movement, twist the cores out of 2 red bell peppers, then halve the peppers and scrape out the seeds. Cut away the white ribs on the inside. Set each pepper half cut-side down on the board, flatten it with the heel of your hand, and slice it lengthwise into strips.
4 Sprinkle the beef strips with about 2 tbsp paprika and toss them until they are well coated. Fry the beef strips in butter and oil in a sauté pan over medium-high heat, taking care not to scorch the paprika.
5 Fry the onions as directed in the main recipe and remove.
6 Sauté the red peppers until tender, 5-7 minutes. Sprinkle over the flour, make the sauce, finish and serve as directed.

VEAL SCALOPPINE WITH SAGE AND PROSCIUTTO

Saltimbocca

🍽 SERVES 4 🥣 WORK TIME 20-25 MINUTES ♨ COOKING TIME 10-12 HOURS

EQUIPMENT

chef's knife

metal spatula

rolling pin

parchment paper*

large frying pan

wooden spoon

chopping board   plate

* waxed paper or plastic wrap can also be used

INGREDIENTS

boneless veal scaloppine

prosciutto

white wine   butter

fresh sage leaves

Made from veal scaloppine, the most popular of all veal cuts, saltimbocca means literally "jump in the mouth." The meat is flattened to make the thinnest of tender, delicate slices, which are topped with aromatic sage leaves and paper-thin slices of prosciutto, then quickly sautéed in butter. The pan juices are deglazed with white wine for a simple sauce. The dish is best served with small pasta quills or shells.

GETTING AHEAD

Saltimbocca can be prepared through step 6 up to 8 hours ahead and kept covered in the refrigerator. Do not overlap the saltimbocca, but layer them between sheets of parchment or waxed paper so that they do not stick together. The veal should be cooked just before serving.

ANNE SAYS

"*Prosciutto is a salt-cured, air-dried raw ham, which is always very thinly sliced. You can find it in Italian markets and in many large supermarkets.***"**

ORDER OF WORK

1 PREPARE THE SALTIMBOCCA

2 COOK THE SALTIMBOCCA

SHOPPING LIST

4	boneless veal scaloppine, total weight about 1 lb
4	thin slices of prosciutto or cured ham, total weight 2 ½ oz
12	fresh sage leaves, more for garnish
¼ cup	butter
⅓ cup	white wine
	salt and pepper

1 PREPARE THE SALTIMBOCCA

Flatten veal gently with rolling pin so fibers of meat are not broken

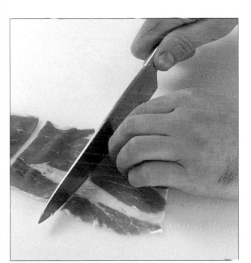

1 Put a piece of veal between 2 sheets of parchment paper. Pound it to a thickness of about ⅛ inch with the rolling pin.

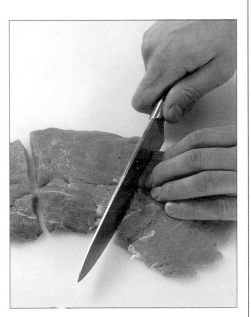

2 Peel the parchment paper away from the meat. With the chef's knife, cut the pounded veal into 3 pieces.

3 Trim away any rind and excess fat from 1 of the prosciutto slices. Cut the slice of prosciutto into 3 pieces.

ANNE SAYS
"The veal shrinks during cooking so the pieces of prosciutto should be a little smaller than the veal pieces."

Center piece of prosciutto on veal

4 Lay a sage leaf on each piece of veal and top with a piece of prosciutto.

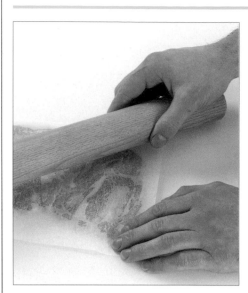

Sage and prosciutto are pressed firmly into veal by pounding

5 Put a piece of parchment paper over the veal and prosciutto pieces, and pound gently to press the prosciutto onto the meat.

6 Peel off the paper carefully so that the prosciutto and sage adhere to the meat. Prepare the remaining veal pieces, sage leaves, and prosciutto slices in the same way.

2 COOK THE SALTIMBOCCA

! TAKE CARE !
Thin veal scaloppine cook very quickly and will be tough if overcooked.

Brown veal lightly so it remains tender

1 Heat the butter in the frying pan. Add a few of the saltimbocca to the pan and brown over medium heat, about 2 minutes.

Browned juices left in pan are basis for sauce

2 Turn each saltimbocca with the metal spatula and brown the other side, 1-2 minutes.

3 As the saltimbocca are cooked, transfer them to the plate and keep them warm.

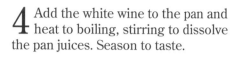

4 Add the white wine to the pan and heat to boiling, stirring to dissolve the pan juices. Season to taste.

ANNE SAYS
"Salt may not be needed because the prosciutto is salty."

Stir up pan juices so they dissolve in wine

Sauce made from cooking juices gives veal a glaze

🍴 TO SERVE

Transfer the saltimbocca to a warmed platter or individual plates using the metal spatula. Spoon the sauce around the veal and garnish with sage leaves.

Fresh sage leaf garnish echoes flavoring in saltimbocca

V A R I A T I O N

VEAL PICCATE WITH MUSHROOMS AND MARSALA

Another favorite veal recipe – these small fried scaloppine are served in a rich mushroom sauce

1 Wipe caps of 8 oz mushrooms with a damp paper towel and trim the stems even with the caps. Set the mushroom caps stem-side down on a chopping board and slice.
2 Set the flat side of a chef's knife on top of 2 garlic cloves and strike it with your fist. Discard the skin and finely chop the garlic.
3 Flatten the veal scaloppine as directed and cut each into 5-6 pieces. Omit the prosciutto and sage.
4 Coat the pieces of veal lightly in ¼ cup flour, seasoned with salt and pepper, discarding the excess.
5 Fry the pieces of veal in 2-3 tbsp butter until browned, 1-2 minutes on each side, cooking them in several batches. Transfer them to a plate.
6 Heat 1 tbsp butter in the pan, add the mushrooms, garlic, salt, and pepper, and cook, stirring occasionally, until the mushrooms are tender, 2-3 minutes. Stir in 3-4 tbsp heavy cream and simmer 2 minutes.
7 Add ¼ cup Marsala, Madeira, or sweet sherry and cook 1 minute longer.
8 Return the veal to the sauce, heat gently 1 minute, and serve. Pasta is an excellent accompaniment.

PORK AND GINGER SUKIYAKI

EQUIPMENT

chef's knife

small knife

strainer   bowls

wooden spoon

slotted spoon

colander   large frying pan

chopping board

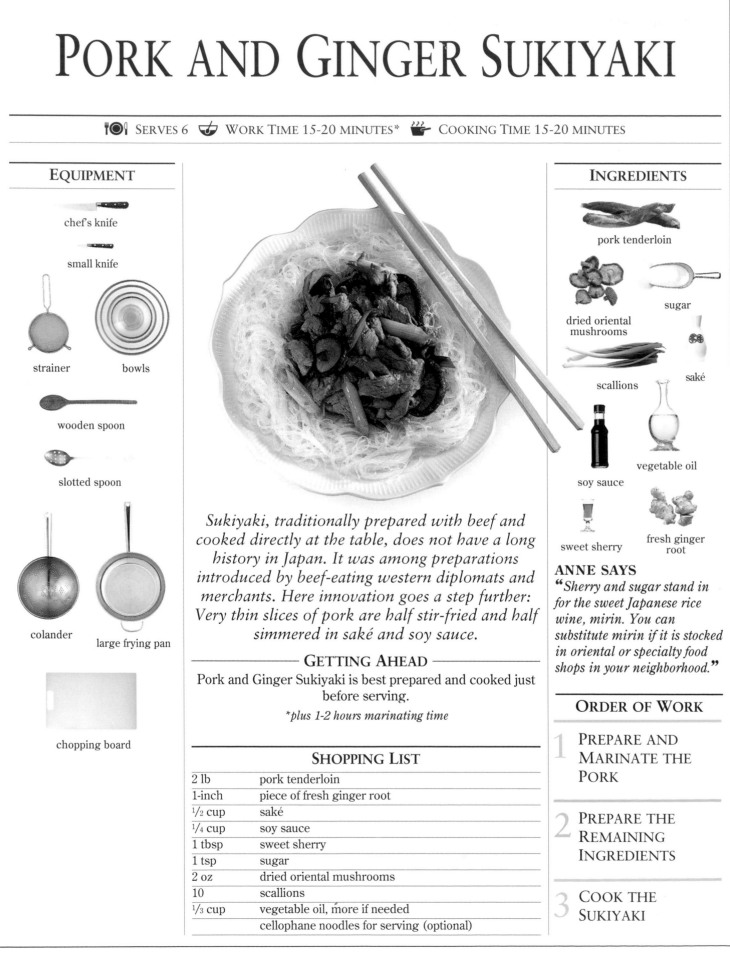

Sukiyaki, traditionally prepared with beef and cooked directly at the table, does not have a long history in Japan. It was among preparations introduced by beef-eating western diplomats and merchants. Here innovation goes a step further: Very thin slices of pork are half stir-fried and half simmered in saké and soy sauce.

GETTING AHEAD

Pork and Ginger Sukiyaki is best prepared and cooked just before serving.

plus 1-2 hours marinating time

SHOPPING LIST

2 lb	pork tenderloin
1-inch	piece of fresh ginger root
1/2 cup	saké
1/4 cup	soy sauce
1 tbsp	sweet sherry
1 tsp	sugar
2 oz	dried oriental mushrooms
10	scallions
1/3 cup	vegetable oil, more if needed
	cellophane noodles for serving (optional)

INGREDIENTS

pork tenderloin

dried oriental mushrooms

sugar

scallions

saké

soy sauce

vegetable oil

sweet sherry

fresh ginger root

ANNE SAYS

"Sherry and sugar stand in for the sweet Japanese rice wine, mirin. You can substitute mirin if it is stocked in oriental or specialty food shops in your neighborhood."

ORDER OF WORK

1 PREPARE AND MARINATE THE PORK

2 PREPARE THE REMAINING INGREDIENTS

3 COOK THE SUKIYAKI

1 PREPARE AND MARINATE THE PORK

Thin, uniform slices ensure that meat cooks quickly and evenly

1 Using the chef's knife, trim the pork tenderloins of any fat and membrane. With the same knife, cut diagonally across each pork tenderloin to make thin, even slices.

Be sure knife is sharp for easy slicing

2 Coarsely chop the ginger (see box, below). Combine the ginger, saké, soy sauce, sweet sherry, and sugar in a non-metallic bowl.

3 Add the pork slices to the bowl and stir so all the slices are coated with the marinade. Cover and marinate 1-2 hours in the refrigerator. While the pork is marinating, prepare the remaining ingredients.

HOW TO PEEL AND CHOP FRESH GINGER ROOT

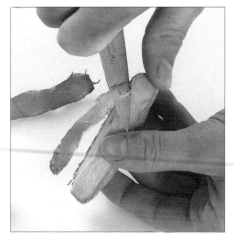

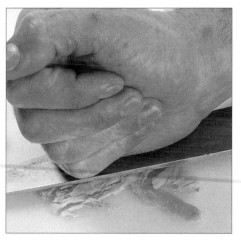

1 With a small knife, peel the skin from the ginger root. Using a chef's knife, slice the ginger, cutting across the fibrous grain.

2 Place the flat side of the chef's knife on the slices of ginger root and crush them by pressing firmly on the blade with your fist.

3 Chop the slices of ginger root coarsely or finely, according to recipe requirements.

2 PREPARE THE REMAINING INGREDIENTS

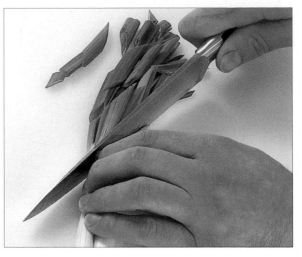

1 Put the dried mushrooms in a bowl and cover with warm water. Soak the mushrooms until plump, about 30 minutes, then drain them well in the colander.

Tip mushrooms into colander to drain

2 Trim the roots and tops from the scallions. Cut the scallions diagonally into 1½-inch pieces.

3 COOK THE SUKIYAKI

1 Heat 1 tbsp oil in the frying pan. Add the mushrooms and scallions and sauté over medium heat, stirring often, until they soften, 2-3 minutes. Transfer to a large bowl. Drain the pork in the strainer, reserving the liquid.

2 Heat another 1 tbsp of oil in the pan. Add one-quarter of the pork and sauté over very high heat, stirring constantly, until the meat is lightly colored, 2-3 minutes.

3 Transfer the cooked pork to the bowl containing the mushrooms and scallions. Cook the remaining pork in batches, adding more oil to the pan as needed.

4 Pour the reserved marinade into the pan. Return the mushrooms, scallions, and pork to the frying pan.

Reserved marinade adds flavor

Scallions add vivid green highlights

5 Simmer the mixture in the marinade just until the meat is heated through, 1-2 minutes.

! TAKE CARE !
Do not overcook the pork or it will be tough.

Stir meat and vegetables so they are heated evenly

🍴 **TO SERVE**
Taste and season with more saké, soy sauce, sherry, and sugar, if needed. Transfer the sukiyaki to warmed individual plates, or, if you like serve in a nest of cellophane noodles.

Tender pork slices are flavored with ginger, saké, and soy sauce

Nest of cellophane noodles forms a delicate background

VARIATION

BEEF, GINGER, AND SESAME SUKIYAKI

Here, beef is combined with fresh ginger root, shiitake mushrooms, and sesame seeds, plus sesame oil for fragrance.

1 Trim the fat and sinew from 2 lb beef chuck steak, then slice the chuck steak as directed for the pork.
2 Prepare the ginger and make the marinade as directed, then let the beef marinate, 1-2 hours.
3 Wipe 8 oz fresh shiitake mushrooms with damp paper towels and trim the stems. Cut the mushrooms into 1/2-inch slices. Alternatively, soak 1 1/2 oz dried shiitake mushrooms in a bowl of warm water until they are plump, about 30 minutes. Drain them and continue as for fresh mushrooms.
4 Prepare the scallions as directed in the main recipe.
5 Toast 2 tbsp sesame seeds: Heat a small frying pan over medium heat, add the seeds, and toast, stirring occasionally, until they are lightly browned, 2-3 minutes.
6 Cook the sukiyaki as directed in the main recipe, stirring in 1-2 tsp sesame oil at the end of cooking.
7 Serve immediately on a bed of boiled Japanese noodles, such as udon or soba, arranging the slices of beef, scallions, and shiitake mushrooms decoratively; sprinkle with the toasted sesame seeds.

RACK OF LAMB WITH SAUTEED CUCUMBERS AND MINT

🍽 SERVES 4　🥣 WORK TIME 35-40 MINUTES　♨ ROASTING TIME 25-30 MINUTES

EQUIPMENT

chef's knife

large metal spoon

boning knife　　teaspoon

metal skewer*

small knife　　2-pronged fork

vegetable peeler

wooden spoon

colander

strainer　　aluminum foil

bowls

medium saucepan

frying pan　　roasting pan

chopping board

* meat thermometer can also be used

INGREDIENTS

racks of lamb

cucumbers

fresh mint　　butter

olive oil　　garlic cloves

white wine

beef stock

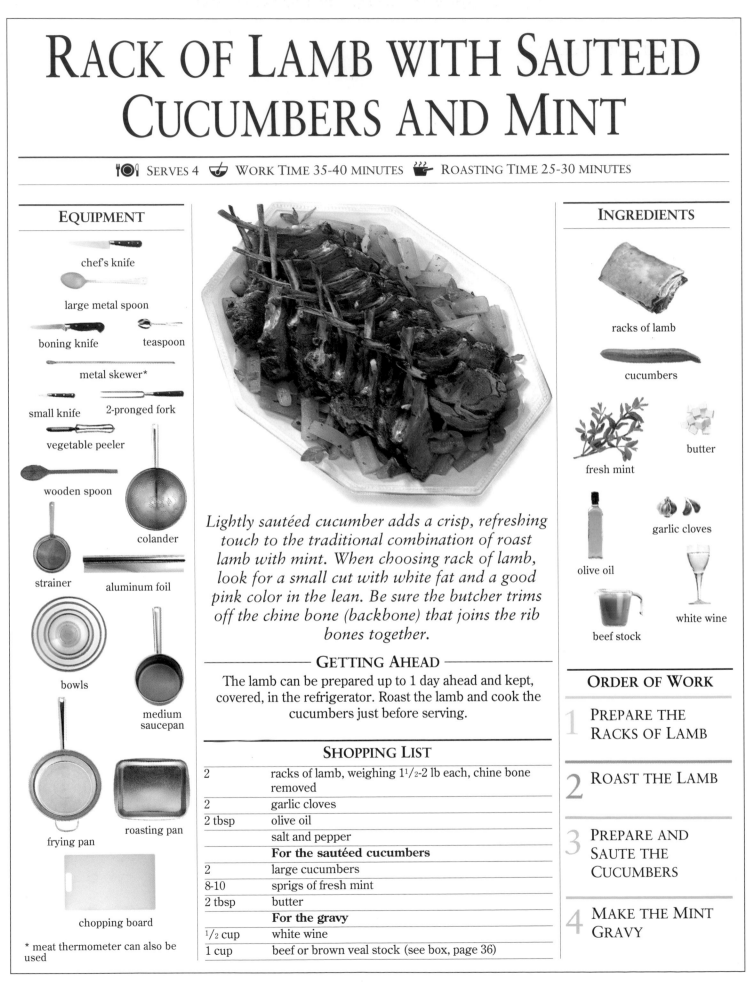

Lightly sautéed cucumber adds a crisp, refreshing touch to the traditional combination of roast lamb with mint. When choosing rack of lamb, look for a small cut with white fat and a good pink color in the lean. Be sure the butcher trims off the chine bone (backbone) that joins the rib bones together.

GETTING AHEAD

The lamb can be prepared up to 1 day ahead and kept, covered, in the refrigerator. Roast the lamb and cook the cucumbers just before serving.

SHOPPING LIST

2	racks of lamb, weighing 1½-2 lb each, chine bone removed
2	garlic cloves
2 tbsp	olive oil
	salt and pepper
	For the sautéed cucumbers
2	large cucumbers
8-10	sprigs of fresh mint
2 tbsp	butter
	For the gravy
½ cup	white wine
1 cup	beef or brown veal stock (see box, page 36)

ORDER OF WORK

1 PREPARE THE RACKS OF LAMB

2 ROAST THE LAMB

3 PREPARE AND SAUTE THE CUCUMBERS

4 MAKE THE MINT GRAVY

1 PREPARE THE RACKS OF LAMB

1 Set a rack of lamb on the chopping board, ribs upward, and, with the boning knife, cut out any sinew lying under the ribs.

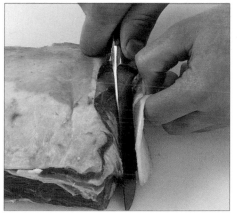

2 Turn the rack over. Cut away the small crescent of cartilage at one end of the rack.

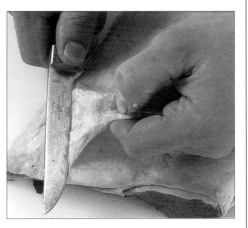

3 Make a small incision under the thin layer of skin covering the fat. Using your fingers, pull off the skin.

ANNE SAYS
"If you can't get a good grip, use a clean dish towel to help."

4 Score through the fat and meat down to the rib bones, about 2 inches from the ends of the bones.

5 Turn the rack over. Place it over the edge of the board and score down to the bone about 2 inches from the ends of the bones.

Thin layer of fat will keep meat moist during roasting

6 Cut out the meat between the bones, using the point of the boning knife. Scrape the bones clean.

! TAKE CARE !
Be sure to scrape away all skin or it will spoil the appearance of the roasted rack.

7 Turn the rack over and cut away the thin layer of meat and most of the fat, if necessary. Repeat the process for the second rack.

ANNE SAYS
"To save time you may prefer to ask your butcher to prepare the rack."

2 ROAST THE LAMB

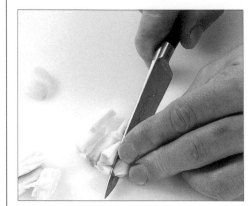

1 Heat the oven to 450°F. Peel the garlic cloves with your fingers, then cut each one lengthwise into 4-5 thin slivers using the chef's knife.

Small knife coaxes little pockets open to allow insertion of garlic slivers

Slivers of garlic add piquant flavor

2 Make several incisions in the lamb with the point of the small knife and insert the garlic slivers in the little pockets, pushing them in with the point of the knife.

3 Transfer the racks to the roasting pan, laying them ribs downward. Wrap the scraped bones in foil to prevent them from being burned. Spoon the oil over the lamb and sprinkle with salt and pepper.

4 Roast the lamb in the heated oven 25-30 minutes, basting the racks once or twice with the juices in the roasting pan. The meat will shrink away from the bones a little during roasting. Meanwhile, prepare and sauté the cucumbers.

5 Test the lamb with the skewer: When inserted in the meat for 30 seconds it will feel warm to the touch when withdrawn. If using a meat thermometer, it should register 140°F.

ANNE SAYS
"Timings and temperatures here are for medium-done. If you prefer your lamb better done, roast it another 5 minutes."

3 PREPARE AND SAUTE THE CUCUMBERS

1 Peel and trim the cucumbers and cut them lengthwise in half. Scoop out the seeds with the teaspoon.

Spoon removes seeds neatly

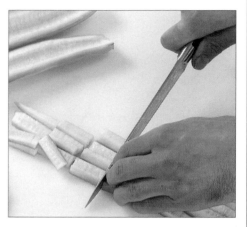

2 Cut the halves lengthwise into 3-4 strips, then gather the strips into a bundle and cut them crosswise into $1^1/_2$-inch sticks.

3 Strip the mint leaves from the stems, reserving a few sprigs for garnish. Set the stems aside for the gravy. Pile the leaves on the chopping board and chop them finely.

4 Fill the saucepan with water and bring to a boil. Add salt, then the cucumber and simmer until just tender, 4-5 minutes. Drain, rinse with cold water, and drain again thoroughly.

Drain cucumber sticks thoroughly

Cucumber should be tender but still firm

5 Heat the butter in the frying pan. Add the cucumber sticks and sauté over low heat, stirring and shaking the pan, until heated through, 1-2 minutes. Stir in the chopped mint and season with salt and pepper.

! TAKE CARE !
Do not overcook the cucumber or it will be bitter.

HOW TO MAKE BEEF OR BROWN VEAL STOCK

Stock is based on raw meat bones gently simmered with aromatic vegetables in water. Ask your butcher to cut the bones into pieces. Boiling should be avoided because it makes the stock cloudy. Season the stock mildly so that it does not overpower dishes to which it is added. For light colored and delicately flavored dishes, use White Veal Stock, which is made using bones that have not been browned.

To make White Veal Stock: *Put 4-5 veal bones, cut in pieces, in a large pot, add water to cover, and bring to a boil. Simmer 5 minutes, then drain the bones and rinse well under cold water. Return the bones to the pot, and add 2 onions and 2 carrots, peeled and quartered, 2 quartered celery stalks and a bouquet garni, 10 black peppercorns, 1 garlic clove, and water to cover. Continue as for the brown veal or beef stock below.*

🍴 MAKES 2-3 QUARTS

🥄 WORK TIME 20-30 MINUTES

🍲 COOKING TIME 4-5 HOURS

SHOPPING LIST

4-5 lb	beef or veal bones, cut in pieces
2	onions
2	carrots
2	celery stalks
4 quarts	water, more if needed
1	large bouquet garni
10	black peppercorns
1	garlic clove
1 tbsp	tomato paste

1 Heat the oven to 450°F. Put the bones in a large roasting pan and roast until they are well browned, 30-40 minutes, stirring occasionally.

Add vegetables to well-browned bones

2 Peel and quarter the onions and carrots. Quarter the celery. Add the vegetables to the pan and brown, 15-20 minutes, stirring occasionally.

ANNE SAYS
"Thorough browning of the bones and vegetables gives the stock flavor and brown color."

3 Transfer the bones and vegetables to a stockpot with a slotted spoon. Discard the fat from the roasting pan and add 2 cups of the water. Bring to a boil, stirring to dissolve the pan juices.

4 Add the liquid to the stockpot with the remaining ingredients and enough water just to cover the bones. Bring slowly to a boil, skimming often. Lower the heat. Simmer very gently, uncovered, 4-5 hours, skimming occasionally. Add water if necessary.

5 Strain and taste the stock. If the flavor is not strong enough, boil the stock to reduce until concentrated. Let the stock cool, then chill. When cold, the fat on the surface will be solid and easy to discard.

4 MAKE THE MINT GRAVY

1 When the lamb is cooked to your taste, transfer the racks to the chopping board. Discard the foil used to cover the bone tips. Cover the racks with foil and set aside.

Foil will keep lamb warm while you make gravy

2 Discard the fat from the roasting pan. Add the wine to the pan and boil until reduced by half, stirring to dissolve the pan juices. Add the reserved mint stems and the stock; boil until well flavored, 5-7 minutes. Season to taste. Strain and keep warm.

🍴 **TO SERVE** Carve the racks of lamb by cutting down between each rib bone. Arrange the chops on a warmed serving platter and surround with the cucumber. Garnish with the reserved mint sprigs. Serve the mint gravy separately.

Lamb chops arranged this way look spectacular

RACK OF LAMB COATED WITH PARSLEY AND BREADCRUMBS

Here roasted racks of lamb are given a crisp finish with parsley and breadcrumbs. Serve with vegetables, such as carrots and okra, glazed with butter.

1 Prepare and roast the racks of lamb as directed in the main recipe.
2 Omit the cucumbers and mint.
3 Trim the crusts from 4 slices of white bread. Work the slices in a food processor or blender to form crumbs.
4 Chop the sprigs from a small bunch of parsley.
5 Melt 3 tbsp butter in a frying pan, add the breadcrumbs, and cook, stirring, until just golden, 2-3 minutes. Stir in the chopped parsley and season with salt and pepper.
6 Heat the broiler. When the lamb is cooked to your taste, press the breadcrumb mixture onto the surface and baste with the pan juices. Broil until lightly browned, 1-2 minutes.
7 Arrange the racks in a guard of honor, if you like, and make the gravy as directed, omitting the mint. Serve with vegetables and an herb decoration.

MINUTE STEAK MARCHAND DE VIN

🍴 SERVES 4 　🥣 WORK TIME 15-20 MINUTES 　🍲 COOKING TIME 40-50 MINUTES

EQUIPMENT

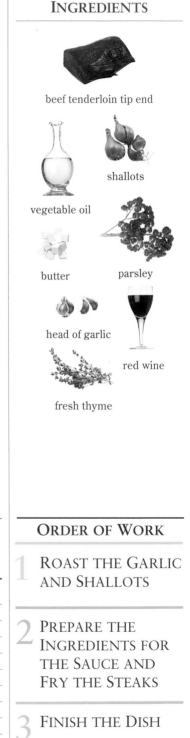

heavy skillet

plate　　　tongs

small baking dishes

large metal spoon

wooden spoon

chef's knife

aluminum foil

chopping board

ANNE SAYS
"A cast-iron skillet is the best to use because it distributes the heat evenly."

In this simplest of all steak recipes, thin "minute" steaks are cut from the tip of the beef tenderloin and pan-fried. Shallots are sautéed in the pan, which is deglazed with red wine for a simple sauce. When roasted, garlic and shallots become surprisingly mild and are the ideal accompaniment, although they can be omitted to save time. Choose a good red wine that you will also want to drink with the meal. Pan-fried steak cries out for classic French fries.

GETTING AHEAD
The garlic and shallots should be roasted and the steaks fried just before serving.

SHOPPING LIST

1	large head of garlic
	vegetable oil, for baking and frying
	salt and pepper
10	small shallots
1	small bunch of parsley
2-3	sprigs of fresh thyme
1½ lb	beef tenderloin tip end
1 cup	red wine
2 tbsp	butter

INGREDIENTS

beef tenderloin tip end

shallots

vegetable oil

butter　　parsley

head of garlic

red wine

fresh thyme

ORDER OF WORK

1 ROAST THE GARLIC AND SHALLOTS

2 PREPARE THE INGREDIENTS FOR THE SAUCE AND FRY THE STEAKS

3 FINISH THE DISH

1 ROAST THE GARLIC AND SHALLOTS

1 Heat the oven to 325°F. To separate the garlic cloves, crush the bulb using your hands to exert pressure. Break the garlic cloves apart, discarding the root.

Sharp blow separates cloves in head of garlic easily

2 Put the garlic cloves in one of the baking dishes, add 1 tbsp oil, and sprinkle with salt and pepper. Stir until they are evenly coated.

3 Trim the roots and remove any papery or loose skin from the shallots, without peeling them. Put the shallots in the second baking dish, setting aside 2 for the sauce. Toss them with 2 tbsp oil, salt, and pepper.

4 Transfer the garlic cloves and shallots to the heated oven. Roast the garlic 30-35 minutes and the shallots 25-30 minutes until tender.

Oil-tossed shallots and garlic cloves roasted in skin are glossy and tender

HOW TO CHOP A SHALLOT

For a standard chop, make slices that are about ⅛ inch thick. For a fine chop, slice the shallot as thinly as possible.

1 Peel the outer, papery skin from the shallot. If necessary, separate the shallot into sections at the root and peel the sections. Set flat side down on a chopping board. Hold the shallot steady with your fingers and slice horizontally, leaving the slices attached at the root.

2 Slice vertically through the shallot, again leaving the root end uncut.

3 Cut across the shallot to make fine dice. Continue chopping the shallot if necessary until it is very fine.

2 PREPARE THE INGREDIENTS FOR THE SAUCE AND FRY THE STEAKS

1 Strip the parsley leaves from the stems and pile them on the chopping board. With the chef's knife, finely chop the leaves. Peel and finely chop the reserved shallots (see box, page 39). Strip the thyme leaves from the stems.

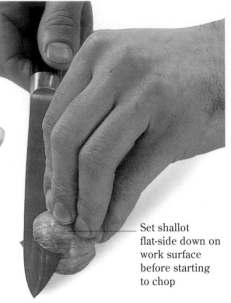

Set shallot flat-side down on work surface before starting to chop

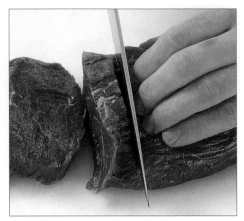

2 Trim any fat from the tenderloin and cut it into 1/2-inch steaks, cutting the steaks slightly thicker at the narrow end of the tenderloin. You should have 8 steaks.

3 Pound the thicker steaks with the flat of the chef's knife so that they resemble the larger steaks. Put the steaks on the plate and sprinkle both sides with salt and pepper.

4 Heat about 1 tbsp oil in the skillet; fry 4 steaks over moderately high heat until well browned on 1 side, 1-2 minutes. Turn them with the tongs; continue frying until well browned but still pink in the center, 1-2 minutes longer.

5 The steaks are done when they yield if pressed with your finger. If firm, they are well-done. Transfer the steaks to a plate, cover with foil to keep warm, and fry the remaining 4 steaks, adding another tablespoon of oil to the skillet. Transfer them to the plate, cover, and keep warm.

Pressing with your finger is best test for completion of cooking

3 FINISH THE DISH

1 Add the chopped shallots to the pan and sauté, stirring, until soft but not brown, 1-2 minutes. Add the red wine and thyme and bring to a boil, stirring. Boil until slightly thickened and concentrated in flavor, 3-5 minutes.

Add parsley to sauce at end of cooking so it retains color and aroma

2 Stir in most of the parsley and taste for seasoning. Add the butter and swirl the sauce, taking the pan on and off the heat, so that the butter thickens the sauce without melting to oil.

3 Put 1 or 2 steaks on each plate and spoon the sauce over the steaks.

¶❄¶ TO SERVE

Sprinkle the steaks with the remaining parsley, and chopped salad leaves, if you like. Arrange the garlic and shallots around the steaks for diners to peel; serve with french fries.

Steak is plump, tender, and juicy

V A R I A T I O N

MINUTE STEAK DIJONNAISE

In this simple variation, red wine is replaced with white wine and tangy Dijon-style mustard and cream are added to the sauce. Instead of roasted garlic and shallots, the steaks are accompanied by caramelized baby onions.

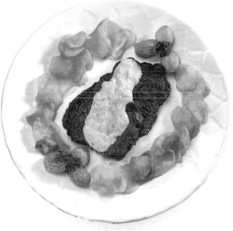

1 Omit the roasted shallots and garlic. Put 20-24 baby onions in a bowl, cover with hot water, and let stand 2 minutes. Drain the onions and peel them with a small knife, leaving a little of the root to hold the onion together. Roast the onions as for the shallots, sprinkling them with 1 tbsp sugar halfway through cooking.
2 Chop 2 shallots. Prepare and fry the steaks as directed.
3 Deglaze the pan with 1 cup dry white wine and boil until reduced by half, 2-3 minutes. Take the pan from the heat and stir in 1 tbsp Dijon-style mustard and 2-3 tbsp heavy cream, omitting the butter. Taste for seasoning.
4 Put 2 steaks on each plate. Coat the steaks with the sauce, set the onions on the side, decorated with parsley sprigs, and serve with home-fried potato chips.

BUTTERFLIED LEG OF LAMB

🍽 SERVES 6-8   🥄 WORK TIME 35-40 MINUTES*   🍲 BROILING TIME 20-30 MINUTES

EQUIPMENT

bowls

boning knife

chef's knife

pastry brush

wooden spoon

metal skewer

2-pronged fork

carving knife

chopping board

Butterflying a leg of lamb is quite simple: The bone is removed and the meat is slit so that it lies flat, and can be broiled in about a quarter of the time that a whole leg takes to roast. The marinade of just oil, garlic, and herbs is delicious, whether the lamb is cooked under the broiler or grilled outdoors on the barbecue. Warm new potatoes tossed with an herb vinaigrette are the perfect accompaniment.

GETTING AHEAD

The lamb can be butterflied and marinated up to 4 hours ahead. It is best broiled just before serving. To serve cold, cook the lamb only until rare and let it cool before slicing.

* plus 1-4 hours marinating time

SHOPPING LIST

1	leg of lamb, weighing about 5 lb
4	garlic cloves
3-4	sprigs of fresh rosemary
3-4	sprigs of fresh thyme
2 tbsp	olive oil, more for broiler rack
	salt and pepper
3 tbsp	red wine

INGREDIENTS

leg of lamb

garlic cloves

fresh rosemary

olive oil

red wine

fresh thyme

ANNE SAYS
"If your broiler is not very hot, brown the lamb first on both sides in a frying pan on top of the stove, then broil 7-10 minutes on each side."

ORDER OF WORK

1 BONE AND BUTTERFLY THE LEG OF LAMB

2 MARINATE AND BROIL THE LAMB; MAKE THE SAUCE

1 BONE AND BUTTERFLY THE LEG OF LAMB

1 Using the boning knife, trim off the skin and all but a thin layer of fat from the lamb. With the pelvic bone upward and using the boning knife, outline the edges of the bones that are exposed.

2 Cut deeper around the pelvic bone, freeing it at the joint and cutting through the tendons connecting it to the leg bone. Remove the pelvic bone. Grasp the tip of the shank (lower-leg) bone and cut all tendons at the base of the bone.

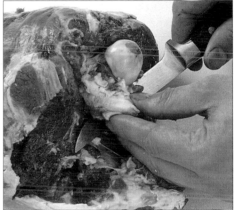

Grasp pelvic bone firmly when cutting meat away

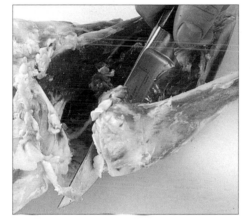

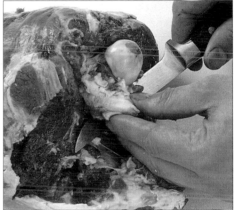

3 Cut the meat away from the shank bone, keeping the meat in one piece. When the bone is clean, locate the knee joint at the point where the shank bone is connected to the leg bone, and scrape away meat and fat to expose the joint.

4 Cut the tendons at the joint and remove the shank bone.

5 With the knife, gently release each end of the leg bone from the meat.

6 Cut and scrape to clean the leg bone, easing it out as you work. Twist the bone and pull it out.

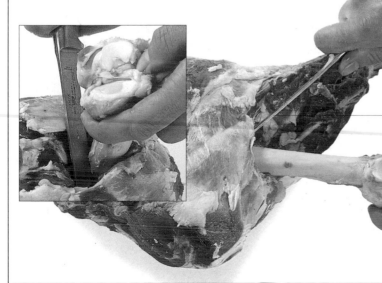

Scrape leg bone with knife to clean away meat neatly

7 Lift and carefully cut away the tendons from the meat.

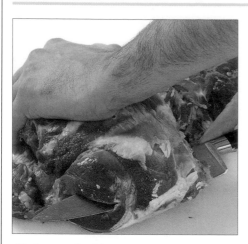

8 Insert the blade of the chef's knife into the cavity left by the leg bone. Holding the blade horizontal, cut outward to slit open one side.

Open out boned lamb

9 Lift up the flap created by cutting open one side, and spread out the meat into a "butterfly" shape.

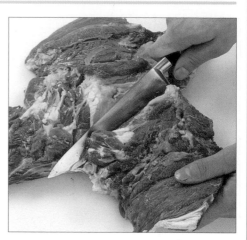

10 Working from the center, make a cut in the thick muscle so the leg can be opened out flat.

MARINATE AND BROIL THE LAMB; MAKE THE SAUCE

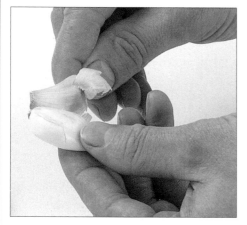

1 Set the flat side of the chef's knife on top of each garlic clove and strike it. Discard the skin and finely chop the garlic. Strip the rosemary and thyme leaves from the stems and chop.

2 Brush the broiler rack and both sides of the lamb with oil. Rub half of the garlic and herbs into the top. Marinate 1 hour at room temperature, or up to 4 hours in the refrigerator.

3 Heat the broiler. Sprinkle the upper surface of the lamb with salt and pepper and broil 3 inches from the heat until brown and slightly charred, 10-15 minutes. Turn the lamb over.

4 Sprinkle the lamb with the remaining garlic, herbs, salt, and pepper, and continue broiling until the skewer inserted in the thickest part of the meat for 30 seconds is warm to the touch when withdrawn, 10-15 minutes. Remove the lamb from the rack, cover loosely with foil, and let it rest in a warm place 5 minutes; reserve the juices in the pan.

Meat will be cooked pink if warm inside when tested with skewer

5 Add the red wine to the broiler pan and heat on top of the stove, stirring to dissolve the pan juices.

Carve meat on diagonal for larger slices

6 Cut the lamb in thick diagonal slices.

🍽 **TO SERVE**
Divide the slices between individual plates and spoon the sauce over the meat. Serve with new potatoes.

Warm new potatoes are dressed with herb vinaigrette

BUTTERFLIED LOIN OF PORK

Like leg of lamb, a loin of pork is a good meat to butterfly. Dijon-style mustard is added to the garlic and herbs to permeate the pork with more flavor and become the basis for the sauce.

1 Butterfly a 3-lb boneless loin of pork: Unroll the flap of meat left from boning and set the pork on a chopping board, fat-side downward. With a chef's knife make a horizontal slit in the meat, cutting almost through to the other side. Open it out like a book.
2 Press the loin into a flat rectangle and cover with parchment paper. Pound it with a rolling pin to tenderize it and achieve an even thickness.
3 Brush the pork with Dijon-style mustard, using about 2 tbsp per side. Sprinkle with double the quantity of oil. Prepare double quantities of chopped garlic and herbs, then rub half into the top of the pork; marinate as directed.
4 Broil the pork 5 inches from the heat, 12-15 minutes. Turn and sprinkle with the remaining garlic and herbs. Broil until a skewer inserted in the thickest part for 30 seconds is hot to the touch, 12-15 minutes longer.
5 Make the sauce as directed, replacing the red wine with white and adding 2 tsp Dijon-style mustard.
6 Arrange slices on a platter, and accompany with the sauce, and with mixed salad leaves, if you like.

LAMB CHOPS IN PAPER CASES WITH FENNEL

🍽 SERVES 4 🥣 WORK TIME 25-30 MINUTES ☕ COOKING TIME 35-40 MINUTES

EQUIPMENT

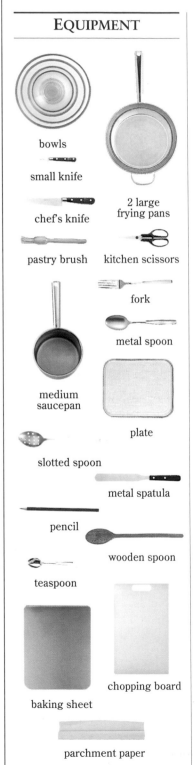

bowls

small knife

chef's knife

2 large frying pans

pastry brush

kitchen scissors

fork

metal spoon

medium saucepan

plate

slotted spoon

metal spatula

pencil

wooden spoon

teaspoon

chopping board

baking sheet

parchment paper

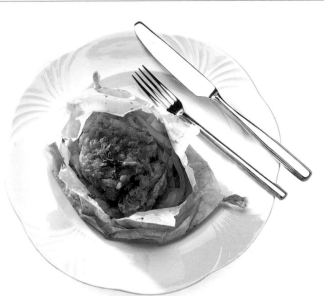

Cooking in a paper case is widely popular, and with good reason. Meats enclosed in parchment steam in their own juices with minimum fat and maximum flavor. Here lamb chops are first browned, then baked in paper on a bed of fennel and tomatoes with a splash of anise liqueur to enhance the flavor. The paper packages puff up golden brown in the oven and make an attractive presentation for each diner to open.

GETTING AHEAD

The lamb chop packages can be prepared up to 2 hours in advance and refrigerated. Bake them just before serving.

SHOPPING LIST

1¹/₂ lb	tomatoes
4	medium fennel bulbs, total weight about 2 lb
2	garlic cloves
¹/₄ cup	olive oil
3 tbsp	pastis
	salt and pepper
4	lamb loin chops, each 1 inch thick, total weight about 1¹/₄ lb
	melted butter for brushing
	For the egg glaze
1	egg
¹/₂ tsp	salt

INGREDIENTS

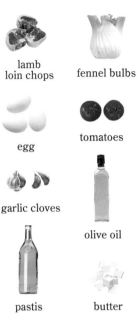

lamb loin chops

fennel bulbs

egg

tomatoes

garlic cloves

olive oil

pastis

butter

ANNE SAYS
Pastis, the French anise- and licorice-flavored cordial, complements the taste of fennel; however, any anise-flavored liqueur, such as anisette, can be substituted.

ORDER OF WORK

1 PREPARE THE VEGETABLES AND LAMB CHOPS

2 MAKE THE PAPER CASES

3 FILL THE PAPER CASES AND BAKE

PREPARE THE VEGETABLES AND LAMB CHOPS

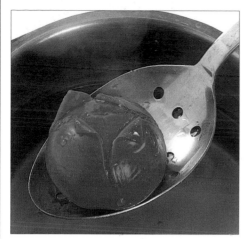

1 Cut the cores from the tomatoes and score an "x" on the base of each with the tip of the small knife. Immerse them in a pan of boiling water until the skin starts to split, 8-15 seconds depending on their ripeness. Using the slotted spoon, transfer at once to cold water.

2 When cold, peel off the skin. Cut the tomatoes crosswise in half and squeeze out the seeds, then finely chop the tomatoes.

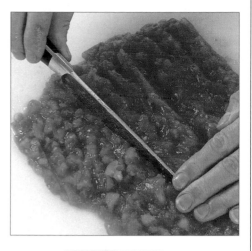

Use sharp chef's knife to cut cleanly through fennel bulb

3 Trim the fennel stems and root, discarding any tough outer pieces from the bulb. Reserve some green fronds for decoration.

4 Cut each fennel bulb lengthwise in half, slicing neatly through the green tops and white bulb.

5 Set each fennel half flat-side down on the chopping board and cut it into thin slices using the chef's knife.

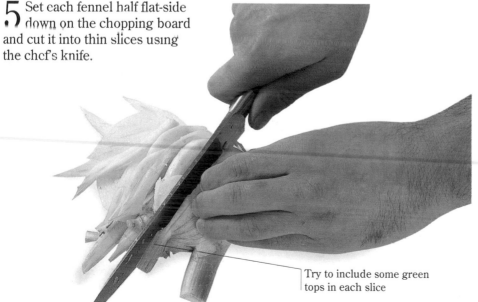

Try to include some green tops in each slice

6 Set the flat side of the chef's knife on top of each garlic clove and strike it with your fist. Discard the skin and finely chop the garlic.

Olive oil adds
Mediterranean
flavor

Add fennel
slices to oil in
frying pan

7 Heat half of the oil in one frying pan, add the fennel and the garlic, and sauté until the fennel begins to soften, 6-8 minutes.

8 Add three-quarters of the tomatoes, the pastis, salt, and pepper to the pan and cook, stirring occasionally, until the mixture is thick and most of the moisture has evaporated, 20-25 minutes. Taste for seasoning.

9 Meanwhile, trim the excess fat from each of the lamb chops. Cut off the "tail" of each. Season both sides of each chop with salt and pepper.

Turn chops with
metal spatula

10 Heat the remaining oil in the second frying pan, add the chops and tails, and cook over high heat until well browned, 1-2 minutes. Turn and brown the other side.

ANNE SAYS
"The chops should only be browned on the outside at this point, to seal in the juices; cooking will continue in the oven."

11 Transfer the chops and tails to the plate and set aside.

2 MAKE THE PAPER CASES

1 Fold a large sheet of parchment paper (about 12 x 15 inches) in half and draw a curve to make a heart shape when unfolded, and large enough to leave a 3-inch border around a chop.

Draw shape lightly with pencil

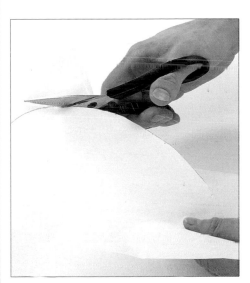

2 Cut out the heart shape with scissors. Repeat to make a total of 4 paper hearts.

ANNE SAYS
"Aluminum foil is a practical alternative to parchment paper for the packages, but the presentation is less impressive because the foil does not puff and brown like paper."

3 Open out the paper hearts and brush each one with melted butter, leaving a border of about 1 inch unbuttered.

4 For the glaze, use the fork to beat the egg with the salt until mixed. Brush the egg glaze on the unbuttered border of each paper heart.

Egg glaze will give airtight seal to packages

3 FILL THE PAPER CASES AND BAKE

1 Heat the oven to 375°F. Spoon a bed of the fennel mixture on one half of a paper heart.

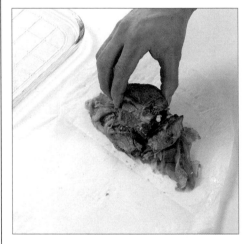

2 Set a lamb chop and tail on top of the fennel mixture.

Fronds from fennel bulbs give anise flavor

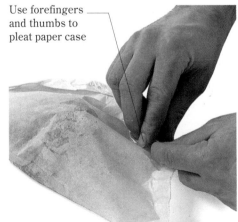

3 Spoon a little of the reserved chopped tomato over the lamb chop and lay a fennel frond on top.

Second half of paper heart will enclose chop and vegetables

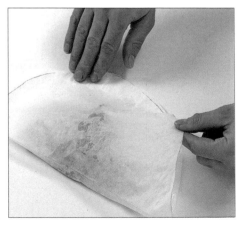

4 Fold the paper over the filling and run your fingers along the edge of the paper to stick the 2 sides of the heart together.

Use forefingers and thumbs to pleat paper case

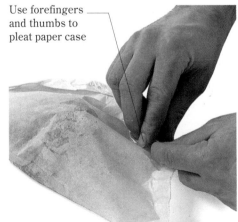

5 Make small pleats to seal the edges of the paper case.

6 Twist the ends of the paper case to finish. Repeat the process with the remaining ingredients to make 4 paper packages.

Arrange paper cases so they don't touch

7 Lay the paper cases on the baking sheet and bake in the heated oven until puffed and brown, 10-14 minutes.

ANNE SAYS
"If the paper packages cool and deflate after being taken from the oven, they can be puffed again by briefly warming them in the oven."

🍽 **TO SERVE**
Transfer the puffed, browned paper packages to warmed individual plates, leaving each person to open his or her own package. Serve at once while the packages are still puffed.

Fennel partners lamb well

Lamb chop and vegetables in paper case make complete meal

LAMB CHOPS IN PAPER CASES WITH LEEKS

Here the lamb chops are baked on a bed of leeks, tomatoes, and herbs cooked in white wine.

1 Prepare the tomatoes and garlic as directed; omit the fennel.
2 Trim 1 lb leeks, discarding the root and the tough green tops. Slit them lengthwise, wash them thoroughly under running water in a colander, drain well, and slice them.
3 Strip the leaves from 3-5 stems of fresh rosemary or thyme, setting aside 4 sprigs for garnish. Pile the leaves on a chopping board and finely chop them with a chef's knife.
4 Heat the oil in a frying pan and add the garlic, leeks, and all the tomatoes with 1/2 cup dry white wine, salt, and pepper. Continue as directed, omitting the pastis. Stir in the chopped herbs at the end of cooking.
5 Brown the lamb chops, make the paper cases, and fill as directed, topping each chop with a reserved herb sprig. Bake and serve immediately.

TENDERLOIN OF BEEF STUFFED WITH MUSHROOMS

🍽 SERVES 8-10   🥣 WORK TIME 50-55 MINUTES*   ♨ COOKING TIME ABOUT 1-1¼ HOURS

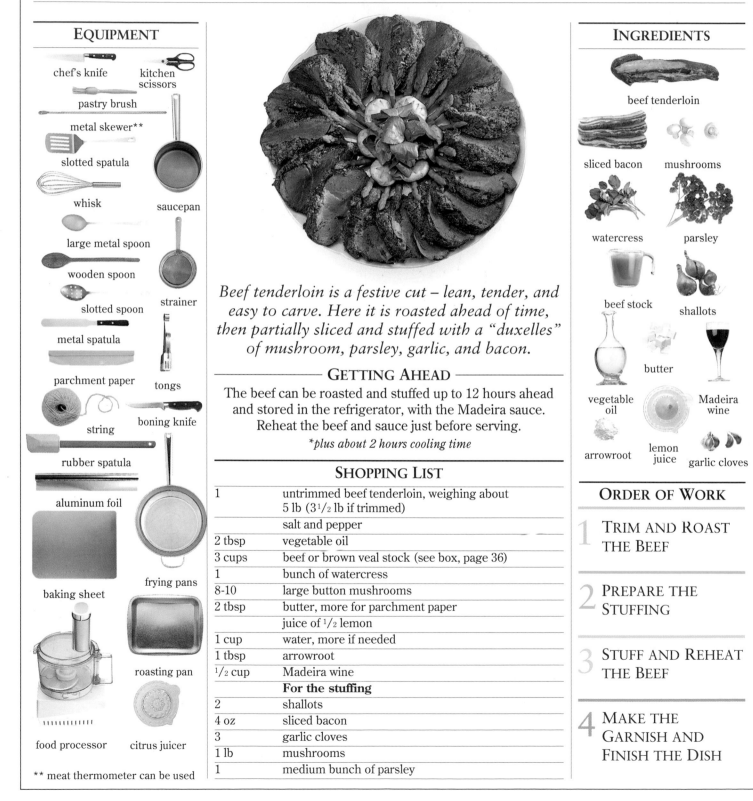

EQUIPMENT

- chef's knife
- kitchen scissors
- pastry brush
- metal skewer**
- slotted spatula
- whisk
- saucepan
- large metal spoon
- wooden spoon
- slotted spoon
- strainer
- metal spatula
- parchment paper
- tongs
- string
- boning knife
- rubber spatula
- aluminum foil
- frying pans
- baking sheet
- roasting pan
- food processor
- citrus juicer

** meat thermometer can be used

Beef tenderloin is a festive cut – lean, tender, and easy to carve. Here it is roasted ahead of time, then partially sliced and stuffed with a "duxelles" of mushroom, parsley, garlic, and bacon.

GETTING AHEAD

The beef can be roasted and stuffed up to 12 hours ahead and stored in the refrigerator, with the Madeira sauce. Reheat the beef and sauce just before serving.

plus about 2 hours cooling time

SHOPPING LIST

1	untrimmed beef tenderloin, weighing about 5 lb (3½ lb if trimmed)
	salt and pepper
2 tbsp	vegetable oil
3 cups	beef or brown veal stock (see box, page 36)
1	bunch of watercress
8-10	large button mushrooms
2 tbsp	butter, more for parchment paper
	juice of ½ lemon
1 cup	water, more if needed
1 tbsp	arrowroot
½ cup	Madeira wine
	For the stuffing
2	shallots
4 oz	sliced bacon
3	garlic cloves
1 lb	mushrooms
1	medium bunch of parsley

INGREDIENTS

- beef tenderloin
- sliced bacon
- mushrooms
- watercress
- parsley
- beef stock
- shallots
- butter
- vegetable oil
- Madeira wine
- arrowroot
- lemon juice
- garlic cloves

ORDER OF WORK

1 TRIM AND ROAST THE BEEF

2 PREPARE THE STUFFING

3 STUFF AND REHEAT THE BEEF

4 MAKE THE GARNISH AND FINISH THE DISH

1 TRIM AND ROAST THE BEEF

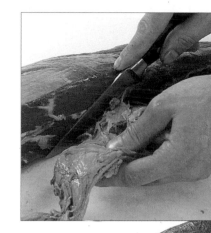

1 Heat the oven to 450°F. To trim the beef, cut and pull away the fat to expose the meat. Cut away the chain muscle that lies to the side of the main part of the tenderloin. Using the boning knife, slit the tight skin of membrane enclosing the tenderloin and cut it away, leaving the red tender meat lying beneath it.

Tough membrane must be removed from tenderloin before cooking

ANNE SAYS
"The chain muscle is tough but can be used, after trimming, for stews or ground beef recipes."

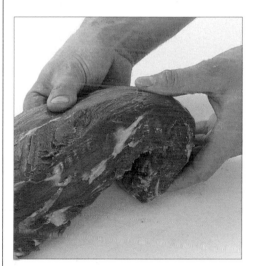

2 If the tail, or tapered end, of the tenderloin is included, fold it under to make an even cylinder of the meat.

ANNE SAYS
"A piece of meat of uniform thickness will cook evenly."

3 Tie one piece of string lengthwise around the tenderloin. Using separate pieces of string, tie the roll at 1-inch intervals.

Pull string to make tight knots

String keeps tenderloin roll in neat shape during cooking

Turn with tongs so meat isn't pierced

Sear meat to seal outside so interior remains moist and juicy

4 Sprinkle the beef with salt and pepper. To sear the meat, heat the oil in the large roasting pan on top of the stove until very hot, then brown the tenderloin well on all sides, turning it with the tongs. Transfer the beef to the heated oven.

5 Roast the beef tenderloin, allowing 12-15 minutes for rare meat or 18-20 minutes for medium-done. For rare, the skewer inserted in the center of the meat will be cool to the touch when withdrawn after 30 seconds; for medium-done, the skewer will be warm. Alternatively, test with a meat thermometer: It will register 125° F for rare meat and 140° F for medium-done.

ANNE SAYS
"Cooking time depends on the shape – a long thin tenderloin will cook more quickly than a short, plump one."

6 Remove the beef, let it cool, and then chill it until cold, at least 2 hours. Discard any fat from the roasting pan. Add half of the beef stock and boil, stirring to dissolve the pan juices. Strain the juices back into the remaining stock and set aside.

2 PREPARE THE STUFFING

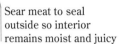

1 Peel the shallots and cut them into quarters. Stack the bacon slices and cut across into about 1-inch pieces. Set the flat side of the chef's knife on top of each garlic clove and strike it with your fist. Discard the skin.

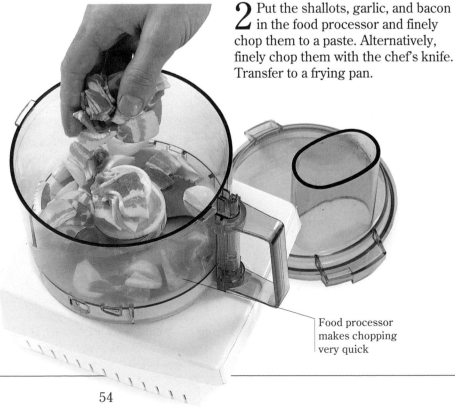

2 Put the shallots, garlic, and bacon in the food processor and finely chop them to a paste. Alternatively, finely chop them with the chef's knife. Transfer to a frying pan.

Food processor makes chopping very quick

3 Wipe the mushroom caps with damp paper towels and trim the stems. Cut the caps into quarters. Chop them in the food processor, using the pulse button. Alternatively, chop them with the chef's knife.

Parsley leaves enhance flavor of stuffing

4 Strip the parsley leaves from the stems and pile them on the chopping board. With the chef's knife cut them into pieces then, holding the tip of the blade against the board, rock it back and forth to finely chop them.

Keep parsley stems for adding to bouquet garni

5 Heat the shallot, garlic, and bacon mixture in the frying pan, stirring with the wooden spoon, until the mixture begins to brown, 2-3 minutes.

6 Add the chopped mushrooms, salt, and pepper and cook over high heat, stirring occasionally, until all the moisture has evaporated, 10-15 minutes.

7 Stir the chopped parsley into the mixture. Taste the stuffing for seasoning. Let it cool, then chill.

3 STUFF AND REHEAT THE BEEF

1 Heat the oven to 425°F. When the beef tenderloin is cold, remove the strings and discard them. Slice the beef at ¹/₂-inch intervals, cutting not quite through the meat so that the underside of the meat remains attached.

2 Set the beef on top of a sheet of heavy-duty foil. With the metal spatula, spread 1-2 tbsp of the stuffing between each slice and press the tenderloin back into its original shape.

Open cuts in meat so stuffing can be inserted

3 Wrap the tenderloin in the foil, making a neat cylinder and twisting the ends of the foil to make handles. Set the tenderloin on the baking sheet and put in the heated oven. For rare beef, allow 15-20 minutes: The skewer inserted in the center of the meat will be cool to the touch when withdrawn after 30 seconds and a meat thermometer will register 125°F. For medium-done, allow 20-25 minutes; the skewer will be warm when withdrawn and a thermometer will register 140°F. Meanwhile, make the garnish.

4 MAKE THE GARNISH AND FINISH THE DISH

1 Rinse the watercress in cold water, drain, and dry thoroughly with paper towels. Discard the stem ends.

Grasp watercress firmly and twist off stem ends

2 Wipe the mushroom caps with damp paper towels; trim the stems even with the caps. With the point of a small knife, make 5 or 6 impressions in the top of each mushroom to create a star design.

ANNE SAYS
"It is easy to make a well-defined indentation in the tender mushroom cap using the tip of a knife, and this is a simple way of creating an attractive garnish with a professional finish."

3 Put the mushroom caps, star-side down, in a frying pan with the butter, lemon juice, salt, pepper, and enough water to partially cover them.

4 Make a paper round: Fold a square of parchment paper in half and then in half again to make a triangle. Fold the triangle over once or twice or more to form a slender cone. Holding the tip of the cone over the center of the pan, cut the cone, using the edge of the pan as a guide. Unfold the round.

Hold paper cone over pan with tip at center

5 Butter the paper round and place it over the mushrooms in the frying pan, buttered-side down. Simmer the mushrooms until tender, 15-20 minutes, then remove them with the slotted spoon and keep warm.

6 Put the stock in the saucepan and pour in the mushroom cooking liquid. Bring to a boil and cook until reduced by half.

Lightly rest edge of baking sheet on rim of pan

7 Put the arrowroot in a small bowl and stir in 2 tbsp of the Madeira wine to form a smooth paste.

8 Whisk the arrowroot paste into the boiling stock. It will thicken at once. Stir in the remaining Madeira wine and taste the sauce for seasoning.

9 Cut a slit in one end of the foil package and drain any juices into the sauce. Whisk the sauce to mix in the juices, then keep it warm over very low heat.

10 Cut open the foil and transfer the beef to a carving board.

Snip down length of foil with scissors

🍴 **TO SERVE**

Cut the tenderloin into slices and arrange on a warmed platter. Garnish with the sautéed mushroom caps and watercress, as well as asparagus if you like, and pass the sauce separately.

Tender beef has rich mushroom filling

Fresh asparagus beautifully complements this elegant dinner party dish

VARIATION

TOURNEDOS OF BEEF WITH MUSHROOMS

Here the beef is cut into steaks – called tournedos – which are seared, then spread with the mushroom stuffing. Instead of the more traditional fried bread, these are served on turnip rounds and topped with the Madeira sauce.

1 Prepare the mushroom stuffing and mushroom garnish as directed in the main recipe.

2 Peel 2-3 large turnips and cut them into 8 rounds, each $1/2$ inch thick. (The rounds should be the same diameter as the tournedos.) Put the rounds in a pan of cold salted water, bring to a boil, and simmer until just tender, 5-7 minutes. Drain thoroughly and set aside.

3 Trim the beef tenderloin and tie it in a cylinder with individual pieces of string. Cut between the strings to form 8 steaks of even thickness.

4 Heat 1 tbsp oil in a large frying pan until very hot. Sprinkle the steaks on both sides with salt and pepper, add them to the pan, and fry until well browned, 3-4 minutes. Turn the steaks with the tongs and continue frying until the steaks are done to your taste. To test, press the top of the steak with your finger; for rare (3-4 minutes on the second side), the meat will yield like a damp sponge; for medium (5-6 minutes on the second side), the meat will resist slightly. If the meat is firm, it is well done and will be tough.

5 Transfer the steaks to a plate and pour off any fat from the pan. Add the stock and boil, stirring to dissolve the pan juices, until reduced by half. Make the arrowroot paste as directed and whisk in with the remaining Madeira wine; taste for seasoning.

6 Put the turnip rounds on individual warmed plates; top with the tournedos. Reheat the stuffing if necessary; spread it on the meat. Set a mushroom on top, pour sauce around the meat, and garnish with watercress. Serve immediately.

ROAST LEG OF LAMB WITH WHITE BEANS

Gigot d'Agneau à la Bretonne

🍽 SERVES 6-8 　🥣 WORK TIME 35-40 MINUTES* 　🍲 COOKING TIME 1½-2 HOURS

EQUIPMENT

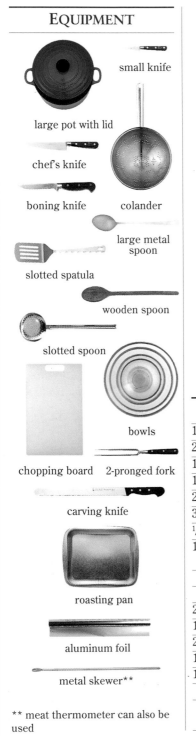

small knife

large pot with lid

chef's knife

boning knife

colander

large metal spoon

slotted spatula

wooden spoon

slotted spoon

bowls

chopping board　2-pronged fork

carving knife

roasting pan

aluminum foil

metal skewer**

** meat thermometer can also be used

A good roast leg of lamb is unbeatable. This version is served Brittany style, studded with garlic and accompanied by white beans. The French would use haricot beans; navy or pea beans are the nearest equivalent.

* plus 8-12 hours soaking time for beans

SHOPPING LIST

1	French-cut leg of lamb, weighing about 6 lb
2	garlic cloves
1	onion
1	carrot
2-3	sprigs of fresh rosemary
3 tbsp	vegetable oil
½ cup	white wine
1 cup	beef or brown veal stock (see box, page 36) or water, more if needed
	salt and pepper
	For the beans
2½ cups	dried white beans
1	onion
2	whole cloves
1	carrot
1	bouquet garni
	2-3 sprigs of parsley (optional)
	baked tomatoes (see box, page 63) for serving (optional)

INGREDIENTS

French-cut leg of lamb

carrots

beef stock　fresh rosemary

garlic cloves

vegetable oil

bouquet garni

white wine

onions

whole cloves

dried white beans

ANNE SAYS

"When choosing a leg of lamb, ask your butcher for a French-cut leg, which is smaller and has had the pelvic bone removed to make carving easy."

ORDER OF WORK

1 SOAK AND COOK THE BEANS

2 PREPARE AND ROAST THE LAMB

3 FINISH THE DISH

1 SOAK AND COOK THE BEANS

Herbs, clove-studded onion, and carrots add flavor to beans

1 Put the dried white beans in a bowl, pour in cold water to cover, and let soak overnight.

ANNE SAYS

"If you are short of time, instead of soaking the beans, put them in a pan, add water to cover, and simmer 1 hour."

2 Peel the onion and stud it with the cloves. Peel and trim the carrot, then cut it into quarters.

3 Drain the beans and put them in the large pot; add the clove-studded onion, carrot, bouquet garni, and enough water to cover by at least 1 inch.

Test bean for tenderness between fingers

4 Bring to a boil, cover the pot, and simmer, skimming as necessary, 1½-2 hours. Add hot water, as needed, to keep the beans covered. Season with salt and pepper halfway through cooking. When cooked, the beans should be tender, but not mushy. While the beans are cooking, roast the lamb.

5 When the beans are tender, remove the onion, carrot, and bouquet garni from the pot and discard them.

HOW TO CHOP HERBS

Parsley, dill, chives, rosemary, tarragon, and basil are herbs that are usually chopped before being added to other ingredients. Do not chop delicate herbs like basil too finely because they bruise easily.

1 Strip the leaves or sprigs from the stems. Pile the leaves or sprigs on a chopping board.

2 Cut the leaves or sprigs into small pieces. Holding the tip of the blade against the board and rocking the knife back and forth, continue chopping until the herbs are coarse or fine, as you wish.

ANNE SAYS
"Make sure that your knife is very sharp, otherwise you will bruise the herbs rather than cut them."

2 PREPARE AND ROAST THE LAMB

1 Heat the oven to 450° F. Using the boning knife, trim off the skin and all but a thin layer of fat from the lamb.

2 Peel the garlic and cut each clove into 4-5 thin slivers. Make several shallow incisions in the lamb with the point of the small knife. Insert the slivers of garlic in the little pockets.

3 Peel and quarter the onion and carrot and put them in the roasting pan. Set the lamb on top. Coarsely chop the rosemary (see box, left). Pour the oil over the lamb and sprinkle with the rosemary, salt, and pepper.

4 Sear the lamb in the heated oven until browned, 10-15 minutes.

ANNE SAYS
"Searing forms a crust around the meat and seals in the juices."

Flavor of rosemary permeates meat

5 Lower the oven heat to 350°F and continue roasting, basting often, 1-1¼ hours for rare meat or 1¼-1½ hours for medium-done. When rare, the skewer inserted in the meat for 30 seconds will be cool to the touch when withdrawn. A meat thermometer will show 125°F. When the meat is medium-done, the skewer will be warm and a meat thermometer will show 140°F.

ANNE SAYS
"If the pan juices start to brown too much, add a little water."

Basting ensures that meat browns and stays moist

BAKED TOMATOES

In Brittany, baked tomatoes are the traditional accompaniment to roast lamb and can be baked while the roast stands.

🍴 SERVES 6-8

🥣 WORK TIME 10 MINUTES

🍲 COOKING TIME 12-15 MINUTES

SHOPPING LIST

3 tbsp	olive oil, more for baking dish
4	large tomatoes, total weight about 2 lb
2	garlic cloves
2-3	sprigs of parsley
½ cup	dried breadcrumbs
	salt and pepper

1 Heat the oven to 375°F. Oil a baking dish. Cut the cores from the tomatoes and cut them in half horizontally. If necessary, cut a small slice off the base of each tomato half so it sits flat.

2 Set the flat side of a chef's knife on top of each garlic clove and strike it with your fist. Discard the skin and finely chop the garlic. Finely chop the parsley. Mix together the garlic, breadcrumbs, parsley, and oil. Season well with salt and pepper.

3 Set the tomato halves in the prepared baking dish and spoon the crumb-herb mixture on each half. Bake in the heated oven until the tops are browned and the tomatoes are tender, 12-15 minutes.

Topping is crisp and golden brown

Cooked tomatoes have tender flesh

3 FINISH THE DISH

1 When the lamb is cooked to your taste, transfer it to a serving platter.

Use slotted spatula and 2-pronged fork to transfer meat

2 Cover the lamb with foil and let stand 10-15 minutes (this will make the meat easier to carve).

3 Make the gravy. Discard the excess fat from the roasting pan, leaving the carrot and onion.

4 Add the wine to the pan and boil the cooking juices and wine until reduced by half.

5 Add the stock and boil, stirring to dissolve the pan juices, until the gravy is concentrated and well flavored, 5-10 minutes. Strain the gravy into a gravy boat and keep it in a warm place.

Stock dissolves caramelized cooking juices to form savory gravy

6 Reheat the beans if necessary. Finely chop the parsley and sprinkle it on the beans, if you like.

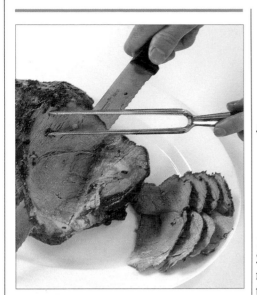

7 Carve the lamb into thin slices using the 2-pronged fork and carving knife.

🍽 TO SERVE

Serve the lamb onto warmed plates. Spoon the beans next to the lamb slices and accompany with baked tomatoes, if you like. Serve the gravy separately.

Roast leg of lamb is carved into lean, juicy slices

Cooking juices are concentrated in flavorful gravy

White beans are classic French accompaniment

LEMON ROAST LEG OF LAMB WITH ZUCCHINI GRATINS

Lemon zest is inserted with the garlic slivers for this roast leg of lamb, which is served with individual baked zucchini and Gruyère custards.

1 Omit the beans and rosemary.

2 Trim the lamb as directed in the main recipe and peel and sliver the garlic. Peel the zest from 1 large lemon with a vegetable peeler and cut half of the zest into pieces the size of the garlic slivers. Cut the remaining zest into fine julienne; blanch in boiling water 1 minute, then drain and reserve for the garnish. Insert 2 pieces of lemon zest with each garlic sliver in the incisions in the meat. Squeeze the juice from the lemon and reserve for the gravy.

3 Roast the leg of lamb as directed.

4 Meanwhile, trim 4 medium zucchini (total weight about 1½ lb) and cut them into ½-inch slices. Blanch in a pan of boiling salted water 1 minute. Drain, rinse with cold water, and drain again thoroughly, patting the slices dry on paper towels. Arrange them in 6 oiled gratin dishes.

5 Grate 1 oz Gruyère cheese. Whisk together 2 eggs, 1 cup heavy cream, three-quarters of the grated cheese, salt, and pepper. Pour the mixture over the zucchini and sprinkle with the remaining cheese.

6 When the lamb is removed from the oven, bake the zucchini gratins until the egg mixture is just set and the tops are golden brown, 10-15 minutes. Meanwhile, cover the lamb with foil and let stand in a warm place until the gratins are cooked.

7 Make the gravy as directed, stirring in the lemon juice just before serving.

8 Sprinkle the reserved lemon zest julienne over the lamb when serving and accompany each serving with a zucchini gratin.

GETTING AHEAD

The beans can be cooked up to 2 days ahead and kept, covered, in the refrigerator; reheat them on top of the stove. It is best not to roast the lamb in advance, however.

ITALIAN BRAISED VEAL SHANKS

Osso Buco

🍴 SERVES 4-6 🥄 WORK TIME 30-35 MINUTES 🍲 BAKING TIME 1½-2 HOURS

EQUIPMENT

2-pronged fork

vegetable peeler

large sauté pan with lid*

chef's knife

grater

small plate

strainer

wooden spoon

bowls

slotted spoon

large plate

chopping board

In this classic dish from Milan, veal shanks are braised with vegetables, white wine, and stock, which form a thick, rich sauce. A zesty mixture called "gremolata" is sprinkled on top just before serving. An excellent accompaniment is risotto Milanese, made with rice, Parmesan cheese, and saffron. Choose thick-cut veal shanks.

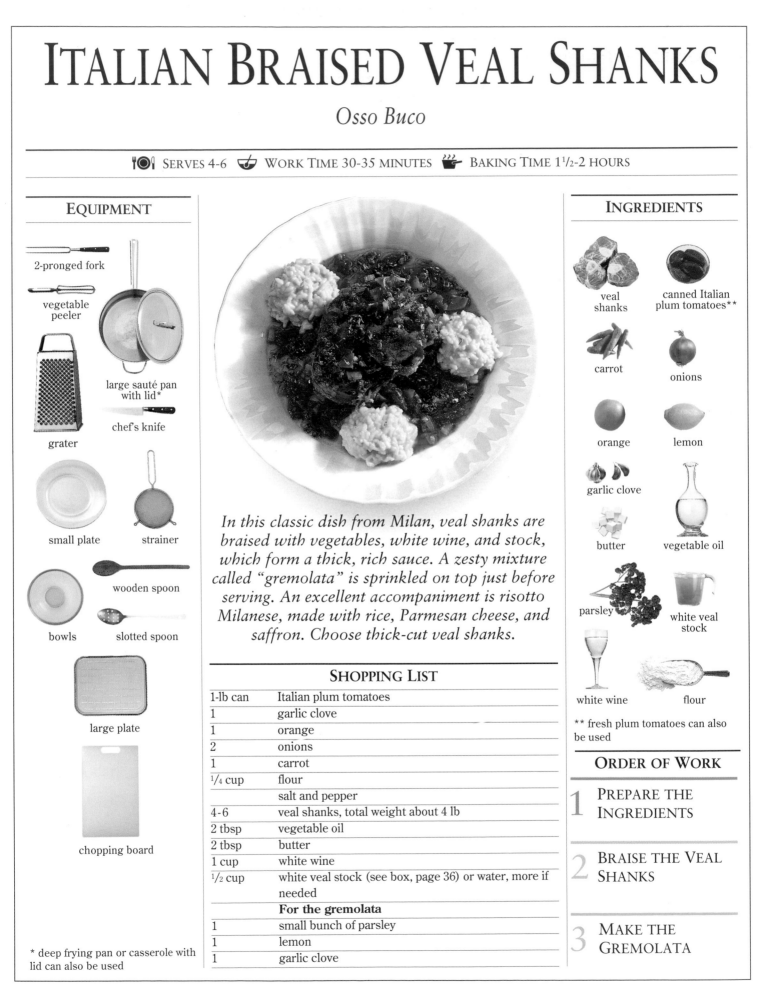

INGREDIENTS

veal shanks

canned Italian plum tomatoes**

carrot

onions

orange

lemon

garlic clove

butter

vegetable oil

parsley

white veal stock

white wine

flour

** fresh plum tomatoes can also be used

SHOPPING LIST

1-lb can	Italian plum tomatoes
1	garlic clove
1	orange
2	onions
1	carrot
¼ cup	flour
	salt and pepper
4-6	veal shanks, total weight about 4 lb
2 tbsp	vegetable oil
2 tbsp	butter
1 cup	white wine
½ cup	white veal stock (see box, page 36) or water, more if needed
	For the gremolata
1	small bunch of parsley
1	lemon
1	garlic clove

ORDER OF WORK

1 PREPARE THE INGREDIENTS

2 BRAISE THE VEAL SHANKS

3 MAKE THE GREMOLATA

* deep frying pan or casserole with lid can also be used

1 PREPARE THE INGREDIENTS

1 Heat the oven to 350° F. Tip the canned tomatoes into the strainer set over a bowl and drain off as much of their liquid as possible. Transfer the drained tomatoes to the chopping board and coarsely chop them with the chef's knife.

ANNE SAYS
"*If using fresh tomatoes, cut out the cores and score an "x" on the base of each. Immerse in boiling water until the skin starts to split. Transfer at once to cold water. When cold, peel off the skin, cut crosswise in half, and squeeze out the seeds. Chop coarsely.*"

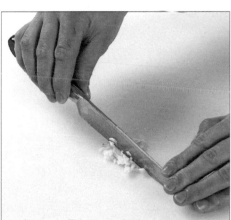

2 Set the flat side of the chef's knife on top of the garlic clove and strike it with your fist. Discard the skin and finely chop the garlic.

3 Grate the zest from the orange. Finely chop the onions (see box, page 68).

Guide knife with fingers of your other hand

4 Peel and trim the carrot. Cut it lengthwise into quarters and then across into thin slices.

Flour coating will seal in juices during cooking

5 Put the flour on a large plate, season it with salt and pepper, and stir to combine. Lightly coat the veal rounds with the seasoned flour, patting to ensure flour adheres.

HOW TO CHOP AN ONION

The size of dice when chopping an onion depends on the thickness of the initial slices. For a standard size, make slices that are about 1/4 inch thick. For finely chopped onions, slice as thinly as possible.

1 Peel the onion and trim the top; leave a little of the root attached. Cut the onion lengthwise in half, through root and stem.

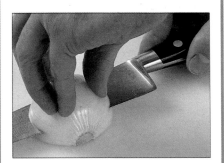

2 Put one onion half, cut-side down, on a chopping board. Using a chef's knife, make a series of horizontal cuts from the top toward the root but not through it.

3 Make a series of lengthwise vertical cuts, cutting just to the root but not through it. Slice the onion crosswise to obtain a dice.

2 BRAISE THE VEAL SHANKS

Veal browns efficiently if pan is not crowded

1 Heat the oil and butter in the sauté pan, add the veal pieces, in batches if necessary, and brown thoroughly on all sides. Transfer to a plate with the slotted spoon.

ANNE SAYS
"The pan should not be crowded or the meat will steam rather than brown, so brown it in batches if necessary."

2 Discard all but 2 tbsp fat from the pan. Add the chopped carrot and onions and cook, stirring occasionally, until soft. Add the wine and boil until it has reduced by half.

Stock keeps veal moist

3 Stir in the tomatoes, garlic, grated orange zest, salt, and pepper. Lay the veal pieces on top.

4 Pour in the veal stock, then cover the pan and cook in the heated oven until the veal is very tender when pierced with the 2-pronged fork, 1½-2 hours. Add more stock during cooking if the pan gets dry. At the end of cooking the sauce should be thick and rich. If necessary, boil to reduce and thicken it.

3 MAKE THE GREMOLATA

1 Strip the parsley leaves from the stems and pile them on the chopping board. With the chef's knife, finely chop the leaves, holding the tip of the knife against the board and rocking the blade back and forth. Put them in a small bowl.

2 Grate the zest from the lemon into the bowl containing the parsley. Chop the garlic and add to the bowl. Stir the ingredients together.

Grate only colored zest from lemon peel

¶◉¶ TO SERVE
Transfer the veal pieces to individual plates, spoon the sauce on top, and sprinkle with the gremolata.

Risotto Milanese brightens this classic dish

Gremolata of parsley, lemon, and garlic enhances taste and color

V A R I A T I O N

BRAISED LAMB SHANKS

In this recipe, called Jarret d'Agneau in France, lamb shanks are cooked in a sauce made with red wine.

1 Prepare the garlic, orange zest, onions, and carrot, as directed in the main recipe; omit the tomatoes. Trim the excess fat from 6-8 lamb shanks (weighing about 12 oz each).
2 Brown the shanks on all sides, then braise as directed, substituting red for white wine, and cooking until tender, 2-2½ hours.
3 Omit the gremolata. Peel, seed, and finely chop 4 fresh plum tomatoes or chop 8 oz drained canned Italian plum tomatoes. Chop 2 garlic cloves and the leaves from 3-5 stems of fresh rosemary.
4 If you like, scrape the ends of the shank bones clean, and arrange like the spokes of a wheel on a serving platter. Mix together the tomatoes, garlic, and rosemary and sprinkle over the meat just before serving.

GETTING AHEAD
The veal can be cooked up to 3 days ahead and kept, covered, in the refrigerator, or can be frozen. Reheat on top of the stove until bubbling; sprinkle with gremolata before serving.

AUNT SALLY'S MEAT LOAF

🍽️ SERVES 4-6   🥣 WORK TIME 25-30 MINUTES   🍲 COOKING TIME 1-1¼ HOURS

EQUIPMENT

boning knife

fork   chef's knife

wooden spoon

metal spatula

metal skewer

9- x 5- x 3-inch loaf pan

bowl

large plate

small frying pan

medium saucepan

plate

food processor

colander

large mixing bowl

meat grinder

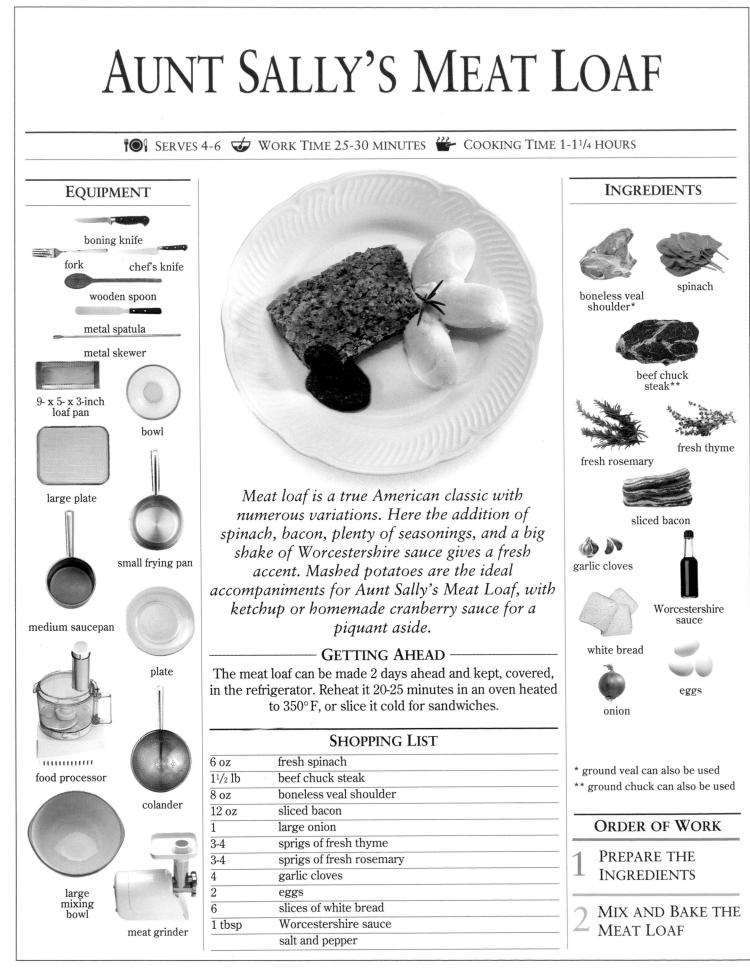

Meat loaf is a true American classic with numerous variations. Here the addition of spinach, bacon, plenty of seasonings, and a big shake of Worcestershire sauce gives a fresh accent. Mashed potatoes are the ideal accompaniments for Aunt Sally's Meat Loaf, with ketchup or homemade cranberry sauce for a piquant aside.

GETTING AHEAD

The meat loaf can be made 2 days ahead and kept, covered, in the refrigerator. Reheat it 20-25 minutes in an oven heated to 350°F, or slice it cold for sandwiches.

SHOPPING LIST

6 oz	fresh spinach
1½ lb	beef chuck steak
8 oz	boneless veal shoulder
12 oz	sliced bacon
1	large onion
3-4	sprigs of fresh thyme
3-4	sprigs of fresh rosemary
4	garlic cloves
2	eggs
6	slices of white bread
1 tbsp	Worcestershire sauce
	salt and pepper

INGREDIENTS

boneless veal shoulder*

spinach

beef chuck steak**

fresh rosemary

fresh thyme

sliced bacon

garlic cloves

Worcestershire sauce

white bread

onion

eggs

* ground veal can also be used
** ground chuck can also be used

ORDER OF WORK

1   **PREPARE THE INGREDIENTS**

2   **MIX AND BAKE THE MEAT LOAF**

1 PREPARE THE INGREDIENTS

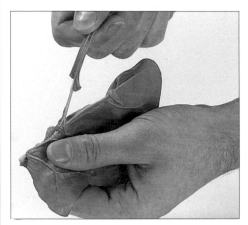

Squeezing removes maximum water

1 Remove tough ribs and stems from the spinach. Wash it well. Half-fill the saucepan with water and bring to a boil. Add salt, then add the spinach and simmer until tender, 2-3 minutes.

2 Drain the spinach in the colander, rinse with cold water, and drain again thoroughly. Squeeze the spinach with your fist to remove all excess water, then chop.

4 Work the beef, veal, and bacon chunks through fine blade of meat grinder.

Feed cubes of meat into machine in small batches

3 If using chuck steak and veal shoulder, trim them of any fat and sinew. Cut the beef, veal, and bacon into large chunks, reserving 4 bacon slices for topping the meat loaf.

ANNE SAYS
"You can also use the food processor to grind the meat: Cut the meat into smaller cubes and grind it with short pulses. Do not overwork the meat or it will be tough when cooked."

HOW TO PEEL AND CHOP GARLIC CLOVES

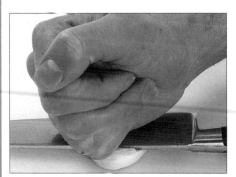

1 To separate the bulb, crush with the heel of your hand. Or, pull out a clove with your fingers. To peel the clove, lightly crush with the flat of a chef's knife to loosen the skin.

2 Peel off the skin with your fingers. Set the flat side of the knife on top of the clove and strike firmly with your fist.

3 Finely chop the garlic clove with the chef's knife, moving the blade back and forth.

5 Peel the onion, leaving a little of the root attached, and cut it in half. Slice each half horizontally, leaving the slices attached at the root end, then slice vertically, again leaving the root end uncut. Cut across to make dice.

6 Strip the thyme and rosemary leaves from the stems and pile them on the chopping board. With the chef's knife, finely chop the leaves. Peel and finely chop the garlic cloves (see box, page 71).

7 Lightly beat the eggs in a small bowl. Trim and discard the crusts from the bread. Work the bread slices in the food processor or a blender to form crumbs, then tip into a large bowl.

2 MIX AND BAKE THE MEAT LOAF

1 Heat the oven to 350°F. Add the ground meat, chopped spinach, onion, garlic, thyme, rosemary, Worcestershire sauce, salt, and pepper to the large bowl and combine with the wooden spoon or your hands.

Mixture is lightly bound by beaten egg

2 Add the beaten eggs to the mixture in the bowl and lightly mix them in.

3 To test for seasoning, fry a tablespoonful of the mixture in the frying pan until browned on both sides. Taste it and add more seasoning to the remaining meat mixture if necessary. Transfer the mixture to the loaf pan, pressing it down and patting it with the wooden spoon to smooth the top.

Pack mixture tightly into loaf pan for even baking

4 Arrange the reserved slices of bacon on top of the meat loaf.

Test meat loaf for doneness with metal skewer

5 Bake the meat loaf in the heated oven until the skewer inserted in the center for 30 seconds comes out hot to the touch, 1-1¼ hours. Let the meat loaf stand at least 10 minutes in the pan, so the meat reabsorbs the juices and is easier to slice.

 **TO SERVE**

Run a knife around the edge of the pan, unmold the meat loaf onto a chopping board, and cut into 1-inch slices. Transfer to a serving platter and serve hot. Alternatively, let the loaf cool in the pan and serve at room temperature.

Bacon slices are attractive finish

Meat loaf is rich and moist with zesty flavor

VARIATION

PORK LOAF WITH APRICOTS

This sweet and savory variation of Aunt Sally's Meat Loaf contains a layer of dried apricots.

1 Soak 1 cup dried apricots in water to cover until plump, about 15 minutes. Coarsely chop three-quarters of the apricots and cut the remainder in half.
2 Prepare the meat-loaf ingredients as directed, omitting the spinach and bacon, and substituting boneless pork shoulder for the beef chuck steak.
3 Put half of the meat-loaf mixture in the pan and spread the chopped apricots on top. Cover with the remaining meat mixture and arrange the apricot halves on top. Bake and finish as directed in the main recipe.
4 Slice the pork loaf thinly and serve with mashed potatoes.

BAKED FRESH HAM WITH ORANGE

🍽️ SERVES 8-10   🥣 WORK TIME 20-25 MINUTES   🍲 COOKING TIME 3½-4 HOURS

EQUIPMENT

aluminum foil

metal spoon

whisk

citrus juicer

large metal spoon

metal skewer*

metal spatula

paper towels

bowls

2-pronged fork

chef's knife

roasting pan

chopping board

* meat thermometer can also be used

Ham, the leg of the pig, is often synonymous with cured meat, but here a fresh pork ham is baked in a low oven and basted with fresh orange juice. Slices of orange and whole cloves adorn the finished glazed ham. The same recipe is easy to adapt for a cooked regular ham, providing the cure is mild: Bake the ham only 1 hour instead of 3 hours until it tests warm with a skewer, then continue as directed.

GETTING AHEAD

The ham can be baked 1 day in advance, wrapped in foil, and reheated in a 350°F oven for 1 hour. It is also excellent cold.

SHOPPING LIST

1	fresh ham with skin, weighing about 10 lb
8	medium oranges
1 tbsp	Dijon-style mustard
1 cup	dark brown sugar
20	whole cloves
1	bunch of watercress
	For the sauce
¼ cup	Grand Marnier
½ tsp	grated nutmeg
½ tsp	ground cloves

INGREDIENTS

fresh ham

oranges

Dijon-style mustard

ground cloves

watercress

whole cloves

Grand Marnier

dark brown sugar

grated nutmeg

ORDER OF WORK

1 BAKE THE HAM

2 GLAZE THE HAM; MAKE THE SAUCE

3 CARVE THE HAM

1 BAKE THE HAM

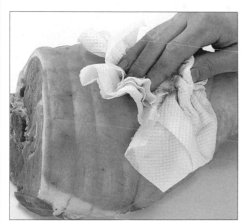

1 Heat the oven to 350° F. Wipe the ham with a paper towel, then set it in the roasting pan.

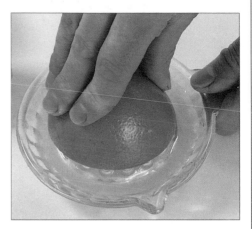

2 Cut 6 of the oranges in half and squeeze out the juice. There should be about 2 cups.

ANNE SAYS
"You can also use store-bought orange juice."

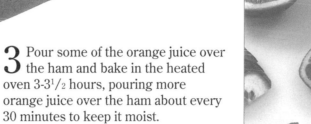

3 Pour some of the orange juice over the ham and bake in the heated oven 3-3$\frac{1}{2}$ hours, pouring more orange juice over the ham about every 30 minutes to keep it moist.

Pour orange juice over whole of ham

4 Meanwhile, cut the remaining oranges in half vertically and cut off the ends. Cut each half into neat slices, discarding any seeds.

Basting with orange juice adds flavor and keeps fresh ham moist

5 To test if the ham is cooked, insert the skewer in the center for 30 seconds; it should be warm to the touch when withdrawn. If using a meat thermometer, it should show 170° F.

! TAKE CARE !
Test in the center of the meat near, but not touching, the bone.

2 GLAZE THE HAM; MAKE THE SAUCE

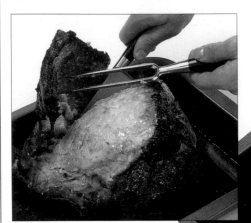

Spoon on sugar and mustard mixture and press onto fat with metal spatula

1 Take the cooked ham from the oven and let it cool slightly. Increase the heat to 400°F. Cut through the skin around the bone end of the ham. With the help of the knife, peel the skin from the fat, starting from the wider end of the ham.

2 Mix the mustard and brown sugar together in a bowl. Spread and press the mixture over the ham, so that it clings to the fat.

3 Overlap the halved orange slices over the ham. Stud each piece of orange with a clove, taking care that the cloves do not break.

4 Continue baking the ham until the surface has a shiny glaze, 30-45 minutes. Baste the ham with the pan juices every 10 minutes, adding more orange juice if needed.

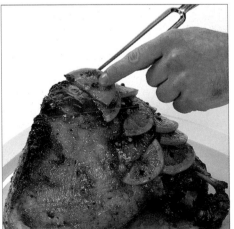

5 Transfer the baked ham to a large warmed serving platter. Remove the orange slices and arrange them on the platter next to the ham. Cover with foil and keep warm.

6 Pour the Grand Marnier into the juices in the roasting pan. Bring to a boil and whisk to dissolve the pan juices. If the sauce is too thick, add more orange juice.

7 Add the nutmeg and ground cloves to the sauce and mix them in with the whisk. Transfer to a sauce boat.

3 CARVE THE HAM

1 Insert the 2-pronged fork in the meat, close to the shank or bone end of the ham. With the chef's knife, make a vertical slice near the shank end, cutting down to the bone, holding the ham steady with the fork. Make 3-4 more vertical slices down to the bone, each about ¹/₂ inch apart.

2 Re-insert the knife at the first slice and curve the knife to slide along the bone, detaching the slices. Continue slicing remaining ham in the same way.

Hold ham steady with 2-pronged fork while slicing

🍴 TO SERVE

Arrange the slices of ham on individual warmed plates with the halved orange slices and add a bouquet of watercress to each. Spoon some sauce over each serving of meat and serve the rest separately.

Glazed ham has delicious fresh sweet accent

Sauce is spiked with Grand Marnier and spices

VARIATION

FRESH HAM BAKED IN CIDER

This ham is basted with apple cider during baking and small apples stuffed with brown sugar and raisins are baked to accompany the ham.

1 Bake the ham as directed, basting with 3 cups non-alcoholic apple cider in place of the orange juice.

2 Omit the halved orange slices. Instead, scrub 8-10 small Golden Delicious apples (total weight about 4 lb) under cold water and remove the core from each with an apple corer or vegetable peeler. Cut a slice from the end of the core and replace it in the bottom of the apple so the filling does not leak out during baking. Score each apple in a horizontal circle with a knife so it does not burst during baking.

3 Remove the ham skin, spread with the mustard and brown sugar mixture, and stud the cloves into the ham.

4 Mix ¹/₂ cup golden raisins with ¹/₂ cup dark brown sugar and stuff each apple. Arrange the apples in the roasting pan around the ham and continue baking to glaze the ham as directed, basting both the ham and apples every 10 minutes.

5 Transfer the baked ham to the serving platter. Make the sauce as directed, adding brandy in place of the Grand Marnier and more apple cider if needed. Add 2-3 more tbsp raisins and simmer in the sauce about 2 minutes.

6 Carve the ham as directed and serve with the baked apples and sauce.

INDIAN BRAISED LAMB

Korma

🍽 SERVES 4-6   🥄 WORK TIME 25-30 MINUTES   🍲 COOKING TIME 2½-3 HOURS

EQUIPMENT

rolling pin without handles

chef's knife

small knife

medium casserole with lid

large metal spoon

metal spoon

chopping board

mortar and pestle*

* spice mill or coffee grinder can also be used

INGREDIENTS

boneless lamb shoulder

dried hot chili peppers

cardamom pods

cinnamon stick

black peppercorns

cloves

ground cumin

plain yogurt

heavy cream

onions

fresh coriander

garlic cloves

vegetable oil

ground mace**

paprika

fresh ginger root

** ground nutmeg can also be used

Korma refers to a fragrant Indian dish in which meat is gently cooked with spices and plain yogurt. Here, the korma is made with lamb.

GETTING AHEAD

Korma can be made up to 3 days ahead and kept in the refrigerator. Add water when reheating, if necessary.

SHOPPING LIST

3 lb	boneless lamb shoulder
6	medium onions, total weight about 1½ lb
1-inch	piece of fresh ginger root
2	garlic cloves
½ cup	vegetable oil
1 cup	plain yogurt
1 cup	heavy cream
	salt
3-5	sprigs of fresh coriander (cilantro)
	For the spice mixture
2	dried hot red chili peppers
5	whole cardamom pods
1	cinnamon stick or 2 tsp ground cinnamon
5	whole cloves
7	black peppercorns
2 tsp	ground cumin
1 tsp	ground mace
1 tsp	paprika

ORDER OF WORK

1 PREPARE THE SPICE MIXTURE AND OTHER INGREDIENTS

2 COOK THE KORMA

3 FINISH THE KORMA

1 PREPARE THE SPICE MIXTURE AND OTHER INGREDIENTS

1 Trim and split the dried hot red chili peppers lengthwise and discard the seeds.

2 Crush the cardamom pods with the flat of the small knife, and extract the seeds with the point of the knife.

3 If using a cinnamon stick, crush it with the end of the rolling pin.

4 Put the chili peppers, cardamom seeds, crushed cinnamon, cloves, and peppercorns in the mortar and crush them as finely as possible with the pestle.

ANNE SAYS
"*If you use a coffee grinder, wipe it well before and after grinding the spices.*"

5 Stir in the cumin, mace, paprika, and ground cinnamon, if using.

Mix ground spices into freshly crushed spices

6 Trim any fat and sinew from the lamb shoulder. Cut the meat into 1-inch slices, then across into 1-inch cubes.

Sharp chef's knife makes cubing meat easy

7 Peel the onions, leaving a little of the root attached, and cut them in half through the root and stem. Lay each onion half on the chopping board and cut across into medium slices.

8 With the small knife, peel the skin from the ginger. With the chef's knife, slice the ginger, cutting across the fibrous grain. Crush each slice of ginger, using the flat side of the chef's knife, and finely chop the slices.

9 Set the flat side of the chef's knife on top of each garlic clove and strike it with your fist. Discard the skin and finely chop the garlic.

2 COOK THE KORMA

1 Heat the oil in the casserole. Add the onions and cook over low heat, stirring occasionally, until soft and golden brown, about 20 minutes. Stir in the ginger and garlic and cook until softened and fragrant, about 2 minutes.

Lightly frying spices develops flavor

2 Add the spice mixture and cook, stirring constantly, until thoroughly combined, 1-2 minutes. Add the lamb cubes to the casserole and cook, stirring and tossing constantly, so they absorb the flavor of the spices, about 5 minutes.

3 Add half of the yogurt, half of the heavy cream, and a little salt, and bring almost to a boil.

4 Reduce the heat, cover, and cook over very low heat until the lamb is tender enough to crush with your finger, 2-2½ hours. Stir occasionally during cooking so the meat does not stick. If the liquid evaporates too quickly, add a little water.

ANNE SAYS
"*Fat from the sauce may separate and come to the surface during cooking. You can spoon off the fat, although traditionally it is served with the korma.*"

3 FINISH THE KORMA

1 Strip the coriander leaves from the stems. Set aside a few whole leaves and pile the remainder on the chopping board. With the chef's knife, finely chop the leaves.

Use fingers to strip delicate leaves from stems

2 Stir the remaining yogurt and heavy cream into the lamb and heat until very hot. Taste for seasoning. Transfer the korma to warmed plates and garnish each serving with the chopped coriander and whole coriander leaves. Serve with rice.

Fresh coriander peps up presentation

Rice topped with golden raisins and toasted pine nuts is an attractive and tasty accompaniment

V A R I A T I O N

MOROCCAN SPICED LAMB

A different spice mixture gives this dish a Moroccan flavor. Serve it with couscous and harissa, the Moroccan hot chili pepper sauce.

1 Omit the spice mixture from the main recipe, and combine the following spices: 1 tbsp paprika, 2 tsp ground ginger, 2 tsp ground cumin, 1 tsp cayenne, and ½ tsp ground turmeric.

2 Prepare the lamb, onions, and 4 garlic cloves as directed; omit the fresh ginger root.

3 Combine the spice mixture with 3 tbsp softened butter and the chopped garlic and rub it over the cubes of lamb. Let stand 30 minutes.

4 Cook the stew as directed, omitting the yogurt and heavy cream and instead adding 1 cup water to the casserole; add more water during cooking if the lamb starts to stick.

5 Meanwhile, heat the oven to 350° F. Spread ½ cup sliced almonds on a baking sheet. Toast them in the heated oven until golden, stirring occasionally, 5-7 minutes.

6 Using a slotted spoon, transfer the lamb pieces to a serving dish or individual plates. Discard the fat from the cooking liquid; boil until slightly thickened, 1-2 minutes. Taste for seasoning and spoon it on the lamb.

7 Make a ring of couscous around the lamb. Sprinkle with the toasted almonds and serve, omitting the coriander.

ROAST RIB OF BEEF PEBRONATA

🍽 SERVES 6-8　　🥄 WORK TIME 25-30 MINUTES　　🍲 COOKING TIME 1¾-2¼ HOURS

EQUIPMENT

chef's knife

small knife

small ladle

teaspoon

slotted spoon

aluminum foil

saucepan

large metal spoon

strainer

plastic bag

metal skewer*

wooden spoon

2-pronged fork

2 frying pans

chopping board

bowls

heatproof baking dish

*meat thermometer can also be used

INGREDIENTS

beef rib roast

parsley

fresh thyme

tomatoes

onion

flour

red bell peppers

red wine

olive oil

juniper berries

garlic cloves

bay leaf

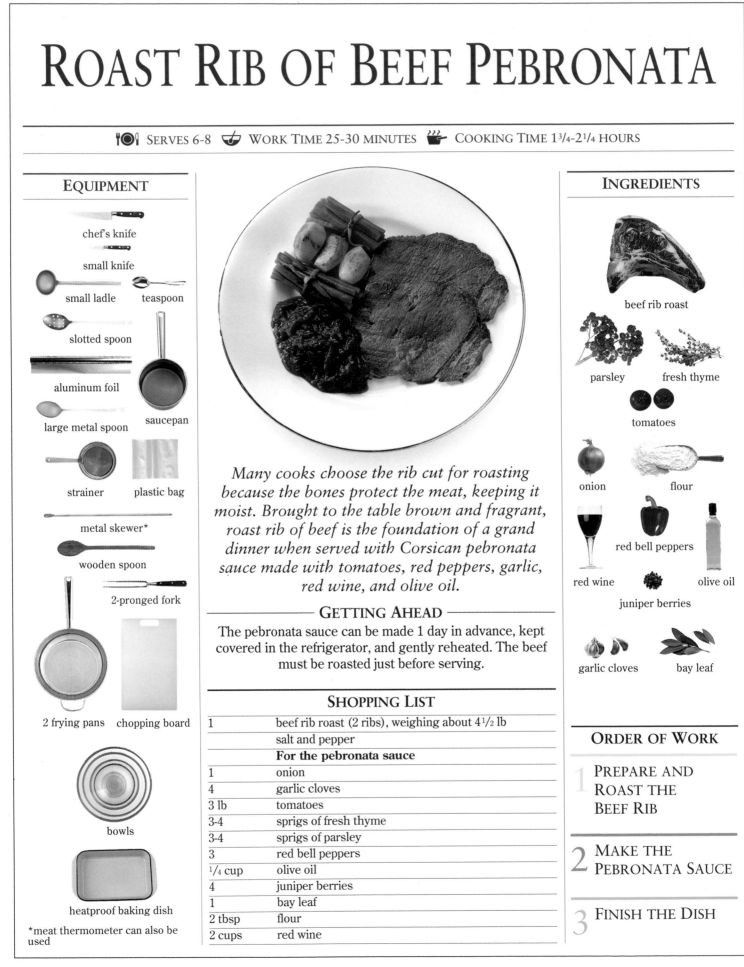

Many cooks choose the rib cut for roasting because the bones protect the meat, keeping it moist. Brought to the table brown and fragrant, roast rib of beef is the foundation of a grand dinner when served with Corsican pebronata sauce made with tomatoes, red peppers, garlic, red wine, and olive oil.

GETTING AHEAD

The pebronata sauce can be made 1 day in advance, kept covered in the refrigerator, and gently reheated. The beef must be roasted just before serving.

SHOPPING LIST

1	beef rib roast (2 ribs), weighing about 4½ lb
	salt and pepper
	For the pebronata sauce
1	onion
4	garlic cloves
3 lb	tomatoes
3-4	sprigs of fresh thyme
3-4	sprigs of parsley
3	red bell peppers
¼ cup	olive oil
4	juniper berries
1	bay leaf
2 tbsp	flour
2 cups	red wine

ORDER OF WORK

1 PREPARE AND ROAST THE BEEF RIB

2 MAKE THE PEBRONATA SAUCE

3 FINISH THE DISH

1 PREPARE AND ROAST THE BEEF RIB

1 Heat the oven to 450° F. Trim the meat, leaving a thin layer of fat to keep it moist. Sprinkle with salt and pepper and set the meat in the baking dish with the ribs pointing upward. Roast the meat in the heated oven until the surface starts to brown, about 15 minutes.

2 Reduce the oven temperature to 350° F. Continue roasting about 1 hour longer for rare beef, or 65-75 minutes longer for medium-done. Baste the meat often with the juices in the dish. While the meat is roasting, make the pebronata sauce.

ANNE SAYS
"If the meat does not produce much juice during roasting, add a few tablespoons of water to the dish."

Carefully trim off most of fat, leaving thin layer behind

3 When the meat is rare, the skewer inserted in the center of the meat for 30 seconds will be cool to the touch when withdrawn. If using a meat thermometer, it will show 125° F. If the meat is medium-done, the skewer will be warm. A meat thermometer will show 140° F.

2 MAKE THE PEBRONATA SAUCE

Finger knuckles guide blade as you chop

1 Peel the onion, leaving a little of the root attached, and cut it in half through root and stem. Lay each onion half on the chopping board and slice horizontally toward the root, leaving the slices attached at the root end, then slice vertically, again leaving the root end uncut. Cut across the onion to make dice.

2 Set the flat side of the chef's knife on top of each garlic clove and strike it with your fist. Discard the skin and finely chop the garlic.

3 Cut the cores from the tomatoes and score an "x" on the base of each with the tip of the small knife. Immerse them in boiling water until the skin starts to split, 8-15 seconds depending on their ripeness. Using the slotted spoon, transfer them at once to a bowl of cold water.

4 When the tomatoes are cold, peel off the skin. Cut the tomatoes crosswise in half and squeeze out the seeds, then finely chop.

Skin is easy to peel off after tomatoes have been scalded

5 Strip the thyme and parsley leaves from the stems and pile them on the chopping board. With the chef's knife, coarsely chop the leaves.

6 Roast, peel, and core the bell peppers (see box, page 85). Cut each half lengthwise into thin strips.

7 Heat half of the oil in one frying pan; add the onion. Sauté, stirring, 3-4 minutes. Add the garlic, thyme, and parsley and sauté 1 minute. Stir in the tomatoes, salt, and pepper and cook, stirring often, until most of the liquid has evaporated, about 25 minutes.

8 Meanwhile, put the juniper berries on the chopping board, set the flat side of the chef's knife on top, and strike the knife blade with your fist to crush the berries.

Crush juniper berries with sharp blow of fist on flat side of knife

9 Heat the remaining oil in the second frying pan, add the red pepper strips, bay leaf, and juniper berries and cook, stirring occasionally, until the peppers are soft, 8-10 minutes.

10 Sprinkle the flour over the peppers and cook, stirring, until lightly browned, 1-2 minutes.

Flour acts as thickener for sauce

Use wooden spoon to combine tomato and pepper mixtures

12 Stir in the onion and tomato mixture and simmer until it is quite thick, 8-10 minutes. Discard the bay leaf and taste the sauce for seasoning.

11 Stir in half of the red wine and bring to a boil, stirring until the mixture thickens. Simmer 2 minutes.

HOW TO ROAST, PEEL, AND CORE BELL PEPPERS

After they are roasted, peeled, and cored, bell peppers can be stuffed whole, sliced and added to salads, or cooked alone or with other vegetables.

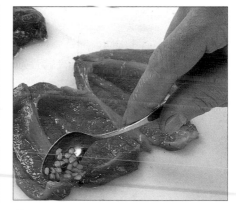

1 Heat the broiler; set the peppers on a rack 4 inches from the heat. Broil, turning once or twice, until black and blistered, 10-12 minutes. Wrap in a plastic bag to trap steam and loosen the skin. Let cool.

2 With a small knife, peel off the skin from each pepper, and rinse the peppers under running water. Pat them dry with paper towels.

3 Cut out the cores. If the peppers are not to be used whole for stuffing, they are easier to seed if first cut lengthwise in half. Scrape out the seeds with a teaspoon.

3 FINISH THE DISH

1 When the meat is cooked to your taste, transfer it to a board, cover it loosely with foil, and leave in a warm place, 10-15 minutes.

2 Tilt the baking dish and spoon off the fat with the large metal spoon. Discard the fat.

ANNE SAYS
"Letting the meat stand allows the juices to redistribute evenly throughout the meat, making it easier to carve."

Wrapping of foil keeps beef warm while gravy is made

Bundles of carrots and green beans are tied with blanched strips of scallion

3 Add the remaining red wine to the baking dish. Bring to the boil, stirring to dissolve the juices in the dish. Simmer 2-3 minutes.

4 Strain into the pebronata sauce. Taste again for seasoning.

 TO SERVE
Carve the beef (see box, page 87), arrange on warmed plates, and if you like, spoon over the juices from the carving board. Add sauce to each plate and pass the remainder separately.

Pebronata sauce brings taste of Mediterranean

VARIATION
ROAST RIB OF BEEF WITH YORKSHIRE PUDDING

The classic British Sunday lunch: Roast rib of beef served with golden batter puddings.

1 Roast the beef as directed in a roasting pan.

2 Meanwhile, make the batter: Sift ²/₃ cup flour into a bowl. Make a well in the center; add 2 beaten eggs with salt and pepper. Slowly whisk ²/₃ cup milk into the center, drawing in the flour to form a smooth paste. Stir in 3 tbsp water. Cover and let stand at least 15 minutes to allow the starch grains to soften so the batter is light.

3 When the meat is done, transfer it to a board and cover loosely with foil. Let stand in a warm place.

4 Increase the oven heat to 450° F. Remove the fat from the roasting pan and pour about a teaspoon into each of 12 muffin cups, adding vegetable oil if necessary. Heat the muffin tins in the oven until very hot, about 5 minutes.

5 Pour in the batter to half-fill the cups. Bake in the hot oven until puffed and very brown, 15-20 minutes.

6 Meanwhile, make the gravy. Stir 1-2 tbsp flour into the roasting pan juices and cook, stirring, until very brown, 2-3 minutes. Add 2 cups beef or brown veal stock or water. Bring to a boil, stirring, then simmer 2 minutes. Strain and season to taste.

7 Carve the roast and arrange on warmed plates with the Yorkshire puddings and vegetables of your choice. Serve the gravy separately.

VARIATION
ROAST RIB OF BEEF WITH GLAZED BABY ONIONS, TURNIPS, AND CARROTS

As an accompaniment for roast rib of beef, glazed vegetables are an ideal winter alternative to pebronata sauce.

1 Roast the beef as directed in a roasting pan.

2 Meanwhile, put 15 baby onions (total weight about 8 oz) in a bowl, pour over hot water to cover, and let stand 2 minutes to loosen the skins. Drain the onions and peel them with a small knife.

3 Trim the ends from 8 oz small turnips and cut them lengthwise into quarters. Using a small knife, round the sharp edges of the turnip quarters and peel away the skin.

4 Peel and trim 8 oz carrots and cut them into 2-inch lengths. Cut broader pieces of carrot in halves or quarters. Round the edges as for the turnips.

5 Put each of the vegetables in a separate small pan and add 1 tbsp butter and 2 tsp sugar to each, with just enough water to barely cover the vegetables. Season with salt and pepper. Bring to a boil, and simmer until the liquid has almost evaporated, 8-10 minutes for the baby onions, 12-15 minutes for the carrots, and 8-10 minutes for the turnips. If the vegetables are not tender when the water has evaporated, add a few more tablespoons water and continue cooking. Shake the vegetables in the pan from time to time so they are evenly coated with glaze.

6 Transfer the roast to a board and keep it warm, 10-15 minutes. Dissolve the pan juices in red wine as directed. Add an equal quantity of beef stock or water and bring to a boil. Taste the gravy for seasoning, then strain.

7 Carve the roast, arrange the slices on warmed plates, and garnish with the glazed vegetables. Spoon over a little gravy and decorate with fresh herb sprigs. Serve the remaining gravy separately.

HOW TO CARVE A RIB ROAST

1 Set the roast upright on the carving board and, holding it steady with a 2-pronged fork, cut away the rib bones at the base of the meat to facilitate carving.

2 With the roast on its side and the knife at a slight angle, carve into ³/₄-inch slices.

PROVENÇAL BEEF STEW

Daube de Boeuf aux Olives Noires

🍽️ SERVES 6-8 🥣 WORK TIME 45-50 MINUTES* 🍲 BAKING TIME 3½-4 HOURS

EQUIPMENT

chef's knife

small knife

casserole with lid

vegetable peeler

saucepans

wooden spoon

fork

colander

slotted spoon

olive pitter

strainer

scissors

kitchen string

bowls

small plate

paper towels

cheesecloth

large plate

chopping board

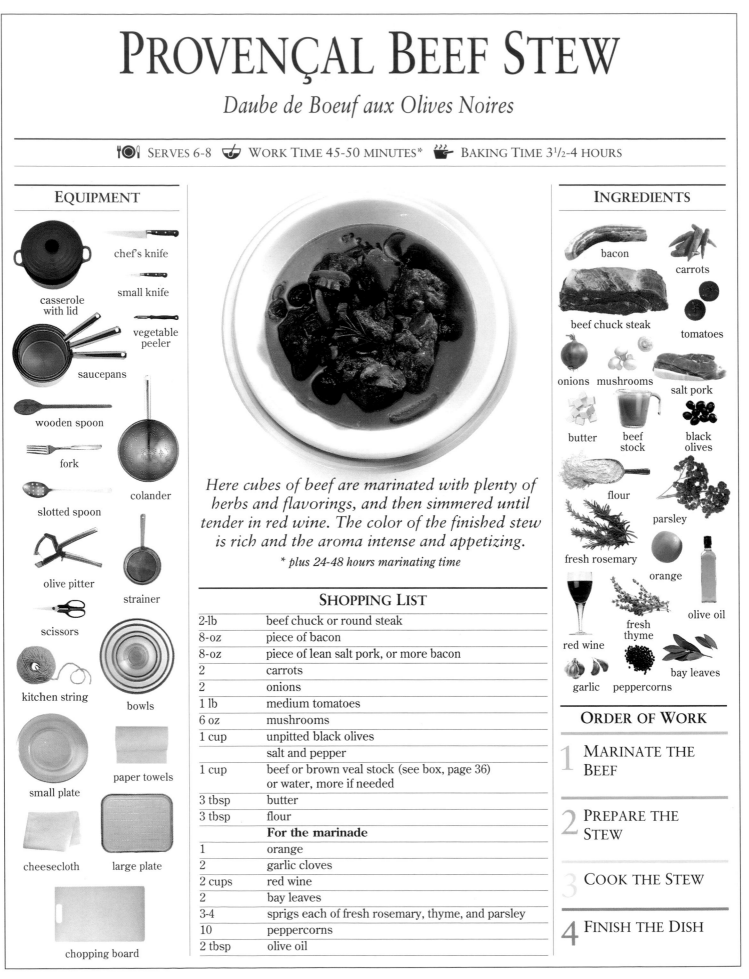

Here cubes of beef are marinated with plenty of herbs and flavorings, and then simmered until tender in red wine. The color of the finished stew is rich and the aroma intense and appetizing.

* *plus 24-48 hours marinating time*

INGREDIENTS

bacon

carrots

beef chuck steak

tomatoes

onions mushrooms

salt pork

butter beef stock black olives

flour

parsley

fresh rosemary

orange

red wine

fresh thyme

olive oil

garlic peppercorns

bay leaves

SHOPPING LIST

2-lb	beef chuck or round steak
8-oz	piece of bacon
8-oz	piece of lean salt pork, or more bacon
2	carrots
2	onions
1 lb	medium tomatoes
6 oz	mushrooms
1 cup	unpitted black olives
	salt and pepper
1 cup	beef or brown veal stock (see box, page 36) or water, more if needed
3 tbsp	butter
3 tbsp	flour
	For the marinade
1	orange
2	garlic cloves
2 cups	red wine
2	bay leaves
3-4	sprigs each of fresh rosemary, thyme, and parsley
10	peppercorns
2 tbsp	olive oil

ORDER OF WORK

1 MARINATE THE BEEF

2 PREPARE THE STEW

3 COOK THE STEW

4 FINISH THE DISH

1 MARINATE THE BEEF

1 Cut the beef into 1½-inch strips, then across into 1½-inch cubes, trimming off any excess fat.

Use chef's knife to cut and trim meat

2 Peel the zest from the orange in wide strips. Set the flat side of the chef's knife on top of the garlic cloves and strike it with your fist. Discard the skin and finely chop the garlic.

Use your hands to mix beef cubes with marinade ingredients to ensure meat is evenly coated

3 Combine the orange zest, garlic, red wine, bay leaves, rosemary, thyme, parsley, and peppercorns in a non-metallic bowl. Add the beef and mix well. Pour the olive oil on top. Cover tightly and let marinate in the refrigerator, turning the beef occasionally, 24-48 hours.

ANNE SAYS
"Oil keeps the meat from drying out."

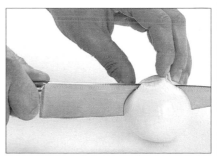

HOW TO SLICE ONIONS

Onions can be cut into thick or thin slices to use in many dishes.

1 Peel the onion, leaving a little of the root attached, and cut it in half through root and stem.

2 Lay each half on the chopping board and cut across into thin or thick slices, as required.

2 PREPARE THE STEW

1 Cut the bacon into ¼-inch slices, discarding any rind. Stack 2-3 slices and cut them into ¼-inch strips; repeat with the remaining slices. Cut the salt pork into dice or strips.

Dice salt pork discarding any excess fat

2 Put the bacon and salt pork in a saucepan of cold water, heat to boiling, and blanch 10 minutes. Drain in the colander, rinse with cold water, and drain again thoroughly.

ANNE SAYS
"This blanching removes excess salt."

3 Peel and trim the carrots and cut them diagonally into ⅜-inch slices with the chef's knife. Peel and slice the onions (see box, page 89).

HOW TO CLEAN AND SLICE MUSHROOMS

Mushrooms absorb moisture quickly, so do not soak them in water. In order to cook evenly, mushrooms should be cut into equal-sized pieces.

1 Wipe the mushroom caps with a damp paper towel.

2 Trim the mushroom stems even with the caps.

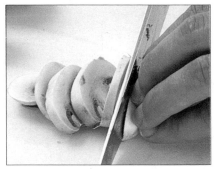

3 Set the mushrooms stem-side down on a chopping board and slice them.

Using olive pitter saves time

4 Score an "x" on the base of each tomato. Immerse the tomatoes in boiling water until the skin starts to split. Transfer them at once to cold water. When cold, peel off the skin. Cut the tomatoes crosswise in half and squeeze out the seeds, then chop each half coarsely.

Pitted olives are left with neat cavity

5 Clean and slice the mushrooms (see box, page 90). Pit the olives.

COOK THE STEW

1 Heat the oven to 300° F. Remove the beef pieces from the marinade, place on paper towels on the large plate, and pat dry; set aside.

2 Strain the marinade. Reserve the liquid and tie the flavoring ingredients in a piece of cheesecloth.

Absorption of marinade darkens meat

Strain to separate marinade flavorings from liquid

3 Spread the bacon and salt pork on the bottom of the casserole and cover with the beef cubes. Layer the tomatoes and onions on top.

Layer vegetables on top of meat

4 Continue layering with the carrots, mushrooms, and black olives. Pour in the strained marinade and the stock and season with pepper. Add the bag of flavorings.

! TAKE CARE !
The bacon, salt pork, and olives will add salt so more may not be needed.

Tender meat is easily crushed in fingers

5 Bring the stew slowly to a boil on top of the stove, then cover the casserole, transfer to the heated oven, and cook 3½-4 hours, stirring occasionally.

6 The beef is ready when it is tender enough to crush in your fingers. Add more stock if the stew seems dry.

4 FINISH THE DISH

1 Make kneaded butter: Using the fork, crush the butter on the small plate. Work in the flour until smooth.

2 Transfer the casserole to the top of the stove and discard the flavoring bag. Add the kneaded butter in small pieces, stirring so it melts into the sauce and thickens it. Simmer 2 minutes; taste for seasoning. Serve in warmed soup bowls. Decorate with rosemary sprigs, if you like.

Black olives star in this succulent stew

Tender beef is ready to melt in your mouth

V A R I A T I O N

PROVENÇAL LAMB STEW WITH GREEN OLIVES

Here, more traditional lamb replaces the beef and green olives are substituted for black olives.

1 Cut 2 lb boned lamb shoulder into cubes, using a chef's knife.
2 Marinate the lamb in the flavorings, 24-48 hours as directed.
3 Prepare the bacon, salt pork, and vegetables as directed, pitting green olives instead of black.
4 Cook the stew as directed.
5 Make the kneaded butter and finish the dish as directed, sprinkling a little chopped thyme on each serving, if you like.

GETTING AHEAD
The stew can be made up to 2 days ahead and kept, covered, in the refrigerator. Reheat on top of the stove until bubbling.

CHILI CON CARNE

🍽 SERVES 6　🥣 WORK TIME 35-40 MINUTES　🍲 COOKING TIME 2-2½ HOURS

EQUIPMENT

large heavy casserole with lid

plate

small knife

chef's knife

saucepan

wooden spoon

slotted spoon

bowls

chopping board

ladle

This chili has cubes of beef browned with onions, garlic, and lots of authentic spices. In Texas, chili's homeland, you will never find a red bean tainting the sacred stew. Instead, red kidney beans and rice are served as accompaniments, with cornbread on the side.

GETTING AHEAD
Chili can be refrigerated up to 3 days and the flavor will mellow. It can also be frozen.

SHOPPING LIST

3	medium onions
3	garlic cloves
1½ lb	tomatoes
2-4	dried hot red chili peppers
5-6	sprigs of fresh oregano or 1 tbsp dried oregano
3 lb	beef chuck steak
3 tbsp	vegetable oil, more if needed
2 cups	water, more if needed
2 tbsp	chili powder
1 tbsp	paprika
2 tsp	ground cumin
1-2 tsp	Tabasco sauce, or to taste
	salt and pepper
1 tbsp	fine cornmeal

INGREDIENTS

beef chuck steak

fresh oregano

tomatoes

vegetable oil

onions

dried hot red chili peppers

paprika

chili powder

fine cornmeal

Tabasco sauce

garlic cloves　ground cumin

ORDER OF WORK

1 PREPARE THE CHILI INGREDIENTS

2 COOK THE CHILI

1 PREPARE THE CHILI INGREDIENTS

1 Peel the onions, leaving a little of the root attached, and cut in half through root and stem. Slice each half horizontally toward the root, leaving the slices attached at the root end, then slice vertically, again leaving the root end uncut. Cut across to make dice.

2 Set the flat side of the chef's knife on top of each garlic clove and strike it with your fist. Discard the skin and finely chop the garlic. Peel, seed, and finely chop the tomatoes (see box, page 96).

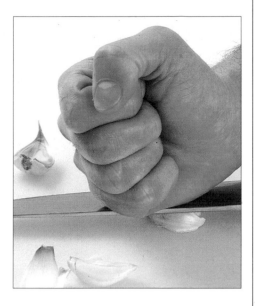

3 Trim and split the chili peppers lengthwise. Discard the seeds, then finely chop or crumble them. If using fresh oregano, strip the leaves from the stems, put in a pile, and chop.

ANNE SAYS
"The seeds are the hottest part of dried red chili peppers; if you like your chili extra hot you can leave them in."

Scrape out seeds with small knife

Chef's knife is efficient tool for cutting meat

4 Trim any fat and sinew from the beef chuck steak. Cut the meat into 1/2-inch cubes.

Cut even-sized cubes so beef becomes very tender in cooking

2 COOK THE CHILI

Browning meat adds flavor to chili

1 Heat half of the oil in the casserole, add about one-quarter of the beef cubes, and cook over high heat, stirring, until browned. Using the slotted spoon, transfer the meat to the plate. Brown the remaining beef cubes in 3 batches, adding more oil as needed.

! TAKE CARE !
It is important to cook the beef cubes in batches so that they brown quickly without giving off much liquid.

2 Return the 3 batches of browned meat, with the juices, to the final batch of meat in the casserole. Add the onions, garlic, and tomatoes and cook, stirring, just until the onions are soft, 8-10 minutes.

HOW TO PEEL, SEED, AND CHOP TOMATOES

Tomatoes are often peeled and seeded before they are chopped so they can be cooked to form a smooth purée.

1 Fill a small saucepan with water and bring to a boil. Using a small knife, cut out the core and stem from each tomato.

2 Turn the tomatoes over and score an "x" on the base of each with the tip of the knife.

3 Immerse the tomatoes in the water until the skin starts to split, 8-15 seconds. Transfer them at once to a bowl of cold water.

Use knife and finger to peel off skin

4 When the tomatoes are cold, peel off the skin from each.

5 Cut the tomatoes crosswise in half and squeeze out the seeds, loosening them with your finger.

6 Set each half cut-side down and slice. Turn the slices 90° and slice again. Chop the tomato flesh coarsely or finely, as needed.

3 Pour in the water, and stir into the casserole with the chili peppers, oregano, chili powder, paprika, cumin, Tabasco sauce, salt, and pepper. Bring just to a boil, then cover the casserole, and simmer until the meat is very tender, about 2-2¹/₂ hours, stirring occasionally.

Chili powder gives zing to dish

Cornmeal thickens chili and adds flavor

4 About 30 minutes before the end of cooking, stir in the cornmeal. At the end of cooking, the chili should be thick and rich.

Red kidney beans are traditionally served separately, but some cooks mix them into the chili

TO SERVE
Taste the chili for seasoning, and serve it hot from the casserole, with boiled white long-grain rice, squares of cornbread, and bowls of red kidney beans.

VARIATION

MEXICAN CHILI CON CARNE

This variation goes south of the border, adding unsweetened chocolate and extra spice to the sauce, to create a Mexican "mole."

1 Prepare the onions, garlic, tomatoes, dried hot red chili peppers, and beef as directed; omit the oregano.
2 Brown the meat, then cook with the onions, garlic, chili peppers, and tomatoes as directed.
3 Add the water, ground spices, and Tabasco with 1 square (1 oz) chopped unsweetened chocolate, 1 tsp ground cloves, and 2 tsp ground cinnamon. Finish as directed.
4 If you like, mix the red kidney beans into the chili, and accompany with avocado slices and tortilla chips.

Meat is tender, juicy, and spicy

BURGUNDY POT ROAST

Boeuf à la Bourguignonne

🍽️ SERVES 6-8   🥄 WORK TIME 25-30 MINUTES   ☕ COOKING TIME 3½-4 HOURS

EQUIPMENT

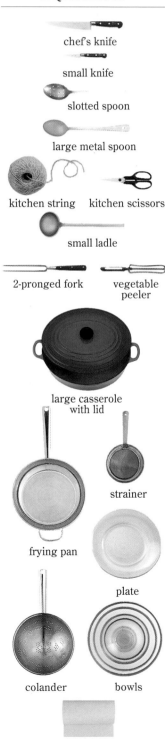

chef's knife

small knife

slotted spoon

large metal spoon

kitchen string   kitchen scissors

small ladle

2-pronged fork   vegetable peeler

large casserole with lid

strainer

frying pan

plate

colander   bowls

paper towels

American pot roast actually has its roots in France because French immigrants who settled in New England introduced their traditional methods of slow-cooking meat to tenderize it. The classic Burgundian garnish of bacon, red wine, baby onions, and mushrooms is delicious with a beef pot roast. Use a rich red Pinot Noir wine.

GETTING AHEAD

Burgundy Pot Roast can be made up to 3 days ahead and kept, covered, in the refrigerator; the flavor improves on standing. Reheat on top of the stove until bubbling.

SHOPPING LIST

1	onion
2	whole cloves
1	carrot
3 tbsp	vegetable oil
1	beef rump roast, weighing 3-3½ lb
1	bouquet garni, made with 5-6 parsley stems, 2-3 fresh thyme sprigs, and 1 bay leaf
1 cup	red wine
	salt and pepper
1 cup	beef stock, more if needed
16-20	baby onions
8 oz	mushrooms
8-oz	piece of lean bacon

INGREDIENTS

beef rump roast*

bacon   beef stock

onion   baby onions

carrot

mushrooms

bouquet garni   cloves

red wine   vegetable oil

* beef round or chuck roast can also be used

ORDER OF WORK

1 COOK THE POT ROAST

2 PREPARE THE GARNISH

3 FINISH THE DISH

1 COOK THE POT ROAST

1 Heat the oven to 325°F. Peel the onion and stud with the cloves. Peel and quarter the carrot.

2 If necessary, roll the beef into a neat shape and, using separate pieces of string, tie the roast at 1-inch intervals to hold the shape.

Browning seals juices into meat

3 Heat 2 tbsp of the oil in the casserole. Add the meat and brown it well on all sides, turning it with the 2-pronged fork.

! TAKE CARE !
The oil must be very hot to sear the meat and seal in the juices.

4 Remove the casserole from the heat, take out the meat and discard all but 2 tbsp of fat from the casserole.

5 Replace the meat in the casserole, and add the clove-studded onion, carrot, bouquet garni, red wine, salt, and pepper. Cover and cook the pot roast in the heated oven 30 minutes.

ANNE SAYS
"Do not add too much salt because the bacon garnish will be salty."

6 Pour in the beef stock and stir well to mix with the liquid in the casserole.

Fork easily pierces fully cooked pot roast

7 Turn the meat over 3 or 4 times during cooking using the 2-pronged fork, and add more stock if too much of the liquid evaporates. Continue cooking about 3 hours. Meanwhile prepare the garnish.

2 PREPARE THE GARNISH

1 Put the baby onions in a bowl, pour over hot water to cover the onions, and let stand 2 minutes.

Little onions are easy to peel after blanching in boiling water

2 Drain the onions in the colander, and peel them with the small knife.

3 Wipe the mushroom caps with damp paper towels and trim the stems even with the caps. Set the mushrooms stem-side down on the chopping board and slice them.

4 Cut the bacon into ¼-inch slices, discarding any rind. Stack and cut into ¼-inch strips. Heat the remaining oil in the frying pan.

5 Add the bacon to the pan, and fry until browned and the fat is rendered (melted down), 3-5 minutes. Transfer to a bowl.

6 Add the baby onions to the pan and cook, stirring occasionally, until lightly browned, 3-5 minutes. Add them to the bacon using the slotted spoon.

7 Add the mushrooms to the frying pan and cook, stirring occasionally, until tender, 2-3 minutes. Transfer them to the bowl containing the bacon and wonions.

All liquid should be evaporated when cooking mushrooms

3 FINISH THE DISH

1 Remove the meat from the casserole. Strain the cooking liquid, discarding the flavorings. If the liquid is too thin, return it to the casserole and boil until reduced and slightly thickened. Return the meat to the casserole with the cooking liquid, and add the bacon, baby onions, and mushrooms. Cover and continue cooking 30 minutes or until very tender.

2 Transfer the meat to the chopping board. Skim any fat from the cooking liquid and taste for seasoning. Remove and discard the string from the beef, then cut into 12 thick slices.

🍽 TO SERVE

Arrange the beef slices on warmed plates. Spoon the garnish and a little of the cooking liquid over the meat. Serve the remainder separately. Decorate each plate with fresh thyme sprigs, if you like.

Bacon garnish
introduces piquant note

VARIATION

FLEMISH POT ROAST WITH DARK BEER

This classic Flemish dish uses beer and lots of sliced onions in place of red wine and the Burgundian garnish. Accompany with braised red cabbage decorated with chopped herbs.

1 Peel 6 onions (total weight about 1½ lb), leaving a little of the root attached, and cut them in half through root and stem. Lay each onion half on the chopping board and cut across into thick slices.
2 Peel and trim 2 carrots, and cut them crosswise into 1-inch pieces. Cut each piece lengthwise into ¼-inch slices. Stack the slices and cut into ¼-inch sticks.
3 Brown the beef as directed. Remove the beef and cook the onions in the casserole over very low heat, stirring occasionally, until soft and lightly browned, 20-30 minutes.
4 Return the beef to the casserole and add the carrots. Continue cooking as directed, omitting the clove-studded onion and carrot for flavoring, using dark beer in place of the red wine, and adding a pinch of ground nutmeg.
5 Omit the bacon, baby onion, and mushroom garnish.
6 Finish as directed, without straining the cooking liquid, but discarding the bouquet garni.

FRENCH HOT POT

Pot-au-Feu

🍽 SERVES 8   🥣 WORK TIME 40-45 MINUTES   🍲 COOKING TIME 3½-4 HOURS

EQUIPMENT

- chef's knife
- small knife
- slotted spoon
- 2-pronged fork
- saucepan
- ladle
- kitchen scissors
- strainer
- vegetable peeler
- kitchen string
- serrated knife
- aluminum foil
- metal spatula
- teaspoon
- knife
- bowls
- cheesecloth
- large pot
- baking sheet
- chopping board

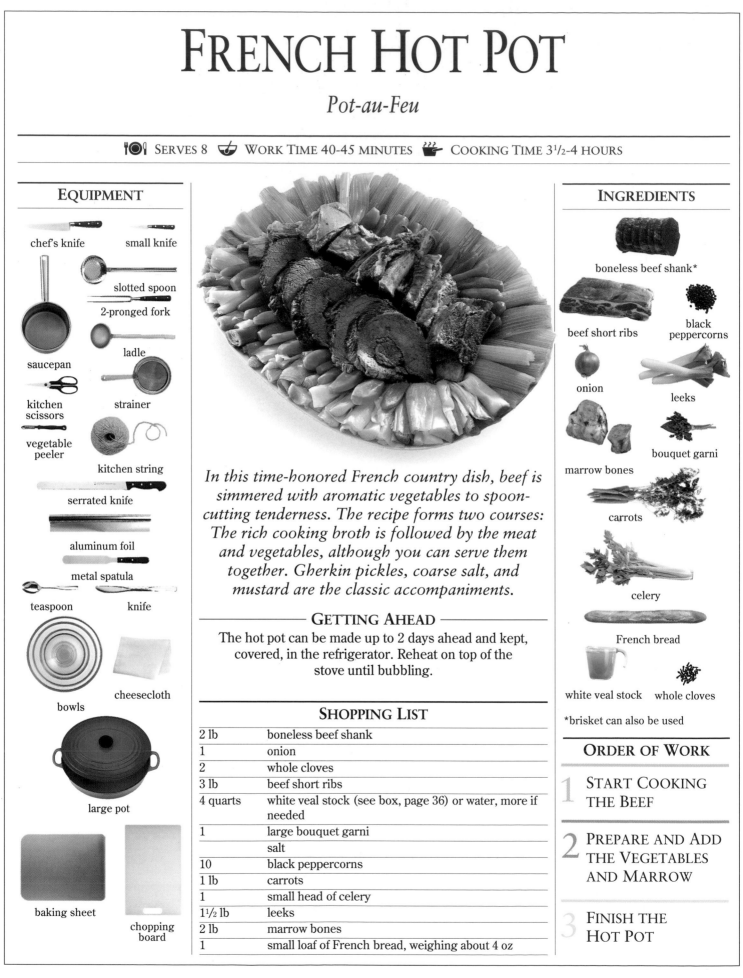

In this time-honored French country dish, beef is simmered with aromatic vegetables to spoon-cutting tenderness. The recipe forms two courses: The rich cooking broth is followed by the meat and vegetables, although you can serve them together. Gherkin pickles, coarse salt, and mustard are the classic accompaniments.

GETTING AHEAD

The hot pot can be made up to 2 days ahead and kept, covered, in the refrigerator. Reheat on top of the stove until bubbling.

SHOPPING LIST

2 lb	boneless beef shank
1	onion
2	whole cloves
3 lb	beef short ribs
4 quarts	white veal stock (see box, page 36) or water, more if needed
1	large bouquet garni
	salt
10	black peppercorns
1 lb	carrots
1	small head of celery
1½ lb	leeks
2 lb	marrow bones
1	small loaf of French bread, weighing about 4 oz

INGREDIENTS

- boneless beef shank*
- beef short ribs
- black peppercorns
- onion
- leeks
- marrow bones
- bouquet garni
- carrots
- celery
- French bread
- white veal stock
- whole cloves

*brisket can also be used

ORDER OF WORK

1. **START COOKING THE BEEF**

2. **PREPARE AND ADD THE VEGETABLES AND MARROW**

3. **FINISH THE HOT POT**

1 START COOKING THE BEEF

1 Tie a piece of string lengthwise around the beef shank or brisket. Using separate pieces of string, tie the beef at 1-inch intervals to form a neat cylinder of meat.

ANNE SAYS
"Tying the meat stops it from curling during cooking."

Tie meat securely so it will hold its shape

2 Peel the onion and stud it with the cloves.

3 Put the shank or brisket, beef ribs, and stock in the pot. Bring to a boil, skimming. Add the onion, the bouquet garni, made with 12-15 parsley stems, 4-5 sprigs of fresh thyme, and 2 bay leaves (see box, below), salt, and peppercorns. Simmer gently, uncovered, 2 hours. Skim occasionally.

HOW TO MAKE A BOUQUET GARNI

This package of aromatic flavoring herbs is designed to be easily lifted from the pot and discarded at the end of cooking.

To make a bouquet garni, hold together the number of parsley stems, sprigs of fresh thyme, and bay leaves required by the recipe. Wind a piece of string around the herbs and tie them together securely, leaving a length of string to tie to the pot handle, if necessary.

Hold herbs firmly together and tie into neat bouquet with string

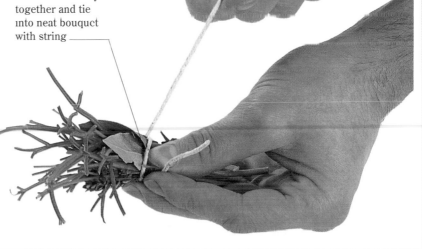

2 PREPARE AND ADD THE VEGETABLES AND MARROW

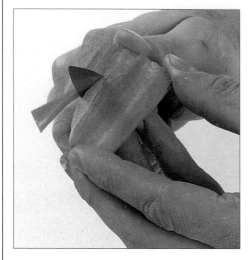

Wrap carrots in cheesecloth so they will be easy to remove from pot

1 Peel and trim the carrots, then cut them into 3-inch lengths. Cut each piece lengthwise in half. Using the small knife, trim the sharp edges to make rounded, barrel shapes.

Use string to secure vegetable package

2 Put the carrots on a piece of cheesecloth, gather up the ends of the cloth, and tie them securely with string to form a package, so that the carrots will be easy to remove at the end of cooking.

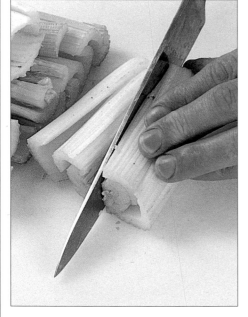

Hold leek leaves apart to rinse out any grit

3 Trim the base and leaves from the celery, if necessary, and discard. Cut the stems into 3-inch lengths and the heart into quarters. Put the celery in cheesecloth and tie with string.

4 Trim the leeks, discarding the roots and tough green tops. Slit the leeks lengthwise in half and wash them thoroughly under running water.

5 Cut the leek halves into 3-inch lengths, put them in cheesecloth and tie with string.

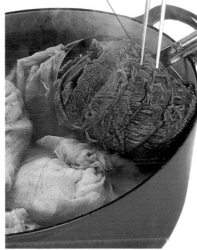

Pierce meat
and vegetables
with 2-pronged
fork to test for
tenderness

6 Put the marrow bones on a piece of cheesecloth, gather up the ends, and tie securely with string.

ANNE SAYS
"The cheescloth package stops the marrow from falling out."

7 Add the bundles of carrots, celery, leeks, and marrow bones to the pot. Add salt to taste. Continue to simmer until the meat and vegetables are very tender, 1½-2 hours longer. Add more stock if needed to ensure that the meat and vegetables are always nearly covered.

3 FINISH THE HOT POT

1 Heat the oven to 350° F. Cut the French bread diagonally into about 20 slices. Arrange the slices on the baking sheet and toast in the heated oven, turning once, until brown around the edges, about 10 minutes.

Turn slices with
metal spatula so
they brown evenly

2 Transfer the meat and marrow bones to the chopping board, cover with foil, and keep warm. Remove the bundles of vegetables from the broth.

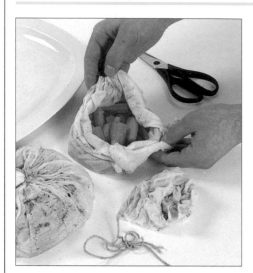

3 Unwrap the bundles of vegetables. Arrange the carrots, celery, and leeks around the edge of a warmed platter, cover with foil, and keep hot.

Reduced broth is pale golden and full of flavor

4 Taste the broth for seasoning and, if necessary, boil it until it is reduced and well flavored.

5 Strain the broth into the saucepan and skim off any fat with the slotted spoon.

6 Discard the strings from the beef shank or brisket and cut it into generous slices. Cut the ribs into pieces, discarding any bones that fall out. Overlap the beef slices in the center of the platter with the ribs alongside, so they are framed by the vegetables. Cover and keep warm.

7 Untie and unwrap the marrow bones, and scoop out the marrow from the bones with the teaspoon.

8 Spread each of the toasted slices of French bread with a little of the marrow.

Marrow adds savor to toast

Marrow-topped toast is rich and satisfying in full-flavored broth

🍽️ **TO SERVE**
Put the toasts in soup bowls, pour over the hot broth, and serve immediately as a first course. Serve the beef and vegetables as a main course, accompanied by coarse salt, gherkin pickles, and mustard.

Pot-au-feu is a warming winter meal

VARIATION

POTEE

Another French classic, this variation of Pot-au-Feu uses pork instead of beef.

1 Tie up a 3-lb rolled pork shoulder into a neat bundle. Put it in a pot with a 1-lb piece of smoked slab bacon, the stock or water, clove-studded onion, bouquet garni, salt, and peppercorns, and simmer as directed.
2 Trim the outer leaves from 1 small head of cabbage (weighing about 2 lb), and cut the cabbage into 6 wedges. Half-fill a large saucepan with water, bring to a boil, add salt, then the cabbage wedges. Blanch 5 minutes; drain, rinse the wedges with cold water, and drain again thoroughly.
3 Omit the marrow bones. Tie the carrots, celery, and leeks in separate pieces of cheesecloth. Add to the broth with the cabbage and finish as directed, cutting the core from the cabbage wedges before serving.
4 Serve the broth with the toasted bread as a first course. Follow with individual servings of pork and bacon accompanied by the vegetables and remaining broth.

PORK NOISETTES WITH CORNBREAD AND CRANBERRIES

🍽 SERVES 4   🥣 WORK TIME 35-45 MINUTES   🍲 COOKING TIME 1-1¼ HOURS*

EQUIPMENT

chef's knife

teaspoon

vegetable peeler

wooden toothpicks

food processor**

bowls

large frying pan

casserole with lid

plate

small saucepan

8-inch cake pan

wooden spoon

slotted spoon

strainer

whisk

2-pronged fork

wire rack

boning knife

pastry brush

metal skewer

**blender can also be used

A stuffing of soft cornbread with crunchy pecans and celery contrasts well with the firm meat of pork, while a cranberry sauce adds a nice balance of tartness. Noisettes are cut from the boned loin and must be very thick to hold the stuffing.

plus 20-25 minutes baking time for cornbread

SHOPPING LIST

1	large onion
1 cup	pecan halves
1	celery stalk
4 tbsp	butter
	salt and pepper
2-lb	boned pork loin
2 tbsp	vegetable oil
1 cup	white wine
6 oz	fresh or defrosted cranberries
2-3 tbsp	sugar
	For the cornbread
¼ cup	butter, more for cake pan
1 cup	yellow cornmeal
1 cup	flour
1 tbsp	sugar
1 tbsp	baking powder
1 cup	milk
2	eggs

INGREDIENTS

cranberries

boned pork loin

celery

yellow cornmeal

vegetable oil

flour

milk

onion

butter

eggs

white wine

pecan halves

baking powder

sugar

ORDER OF WORK

1 MAKE THE CORNBREAD

2 MAKE THE STUFFING

3 STUFF AND COOK THE PORK

4 MAKE THE CRANBERRY SAUCE

1 MAKE THE CORNBREAD

1 Heat the oven to 425°F. Butter the cake pan. Melt the butter. Sift the cornmeal, flour, sugar, 1 tsp salt, and the baking powder into a medium bowl and make a well in the center.

2 Whisk the milk and eggs in a small bowl until combined. Pour them into the well in the dry ingredients and add the melted butter. Mix gently with the wooden spoon until combined.

Wooden spoon speeds up pouring process

3 Pour the mixture into the cake pan and bake until the skewer inserted in the center comes out clean, 20-25 minutes. Let cool; cut into 9 squares.

2 MAKE THE STUFFING

1 Work 2 cornbread squares in the food processor to form crumbs. Reserve the remaining cornbread squares for serving.

2 Peel and chop the onion. Chop the pecans coarsely. Peel the strings from the celery stalk with the vegetable peeler and cut it into thin slices.

Cornbread crumbs help to bind stuffing

3 Heat 3 tbsp of butter in the frying pan, add the onion and celery, and cook, stirring, until soft but not brown, 5-7 minutes. Take from the heat, add three-quarters of the pecans, the cornbread crumbs, salt, and pepper, and stir to combine.

3 STUFF AND COOK THE PORK

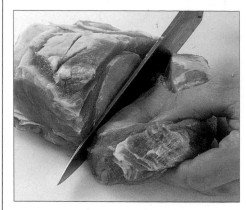

1 Heat the oven to 350° F. Trim any sinew and excess fat from the loin of pork. Cut the loin across into four 1½-inch noisettes with the chef's knife.

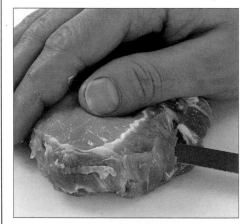

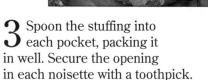

Teaspoon is just right size to insert stuffing into pocket in noisette

2 Using the boning knife, make a deep slit in the side of each noisette to form a pocket. Season the noisettes inside and out.

3 Spoon the stuffing into each pocket, packing it in well. Secure the opening in each noisette with a toothpick.

4 Heat the oil and remaining 1 tbsp butter in the casserole. Add 2 noisettes. Brown them thoroughly on one side, 3-5 minutes. Turn the noisettes over and brown on the other side, 3-5 minutes. Transfer them to the plate with the slotted spoon and brown the remaining 2 noisettes. Return the first 2 noisettes to the casserole.

5 Pour in enough water to come halfway up the noisettes. Cover and cook in the heated oven, turning once, 1-1¼ hours. If the casserole gets dry, add a little more water. The noisettes are cooked if they are tender when pierced with the 2-pronged fork.

! TAKE CARE !
Do not overcook the pork noisettes or they will be tough and dry.

6 Transfer the noisettes to a warmed serving platter or individual plates, using the slotted spoon. Remove the toothpicks from the noisettes, cover the meat, and keep it warm while you make the cranberry sauce.

4 MAKE THE CRANBERRY SAUCE

1 Skim off and discard any excess fat from the casserole; heat the juices to boiling. Boil until reduced by half. Add the wine, cranberries, sugar, salt, and pepper. Bring to a boil and cook, stirring occasionally, until the cranberries pop and are tender, 8-12 minutes.

Add cranberries to reduced cooking juices and wine

🍴 TO SERVE

Sprinkle the noisettes with the remaining chopped pecans. Serve the reserved cornbread, cut into triangles, on the side, and the cranberry sauce separately. Decorate with celery leaves.

Chopped pecans contrast with soft texture of stuffed noisettes

Cornbread accompaniment echoes stuffing of pork noisettes

GETTING AHEAD

The cornbread and stuffing can be made 2 days ahead; keep the cornbread in an airtight container; cover the stuffing, and refrigerate. Stuff the noisettes not more than 4 hours ahead; cook just before serving.

VARIATION

PORK NOISETTES WITH CORNBREAD AND APPLE RINGS

The classic pairing of pork and apples is found in this variation.

1 Strip the leaves from 3-4 sprigs of fresh sage. Finely chop the leaves.
2 Make the cornbread and stuffing as directed, adding the chopped sage with the pecans.
3 Stuff and cook the pork as directed, adding 2 peeled, cored, and chopped tart apples to the casserole 30 minutes before the end of cooking.
4 While the pork is cooking, core 2 medium apples and cut them into medium rings, with the skin.
5 Heat 2 tbsp butter in a frying pan, add the apple rings, and sprinkle with 1 tbsp sugar. Turn them over and sprinkle with 1 tbsp more sugar. Sauté, turning them once, until caramelized and just tender, 3-5 minutes; set aside.
6 Transfer the noisettes to a warmed plate, cover, and keep warm. Discard any excess fat from the casserole; heat the juices to boiling; boil until reduced by half. Add the wine, 1-2 tbsp sugar, salt, and pepper. Cook until slightly thickened, 3-5 minutes. Stir in $1/4$ cup heavy cream, and bring the sauce just to a boil. Transfer to a food processor or blender and purée until smooth. Reheat and taste for seasoning.
7 Serve individual noisettes with a little sauce poured over. Serve with the reserved cornbread, cut with a "daisy" cookie cutter if you like. Garnish with the apple rings, and fresh sage leaves.

STEAK AND WILD MUSHROOM PIE

🍽 SERVES 4-6　　🥄 WORK TIME 50-55 MINUTES*　　🍲 COOKING TIME 2½-3 HOURS

EQUIPMENT

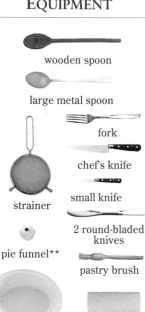

wooden spoon

large metal spoon

fork

chef's knife

small knife

strainer

2 round-bladed knives

pie funnel**

pastry brush

oval pie dish (2 quart capacity)

paper towels

bowls

plate

rolling pin

medium casserole with lid

chopping board

** demitasse cup can also be used

A departure from the quintessentially British steak and kidney pie, this version combines chuck steak with wild mushrooms under a quick puff-pastry crust. The steak is cubed and sautéed, then slowly simmered in a dark sauce with the silky textured wild mushrooms. A deep quiche pan can be substituted for the classic oval pie dish, in which case you will need to increase the dough quantities by half.

GETTING AHEAD

The pie can be baked 1 day ahead and kept, covered, in the refrigerator. Reheat it in a 325°F oven just before serving.

* plus 1¼ hours chilling time

SHOPPING LIST

1 lb	fresh or 2½ oz dried wild mushrooms, such as shiitake or oyster mushrooms
4	shallots
6	sprigs of parsley
2 lb	beef chuck steak
5 tbsp	flour
1 quart	beef stock or water, more if needed
	salt and pepper
	For the quick puff pastry
2 cups	flour, more for sprinkling
¾ cup	unsalted butter
6 tbsp	water, more if needed
1	egg for glazing

INGREDIENTS

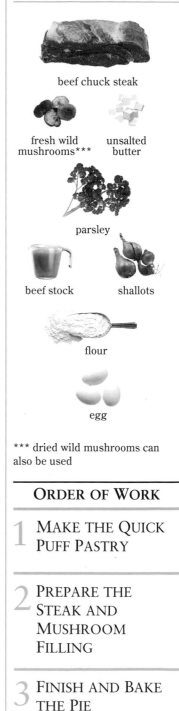

beef chuck steak

fresh wild mushrooms***

unsalted butter

parsley

beef stock

shallots

flour

egg

*** dried wild mushrooms can also be used

ORDER OF WORK

1 MAKE THE QUICK PUFF PASTRY

2 PREPARE THE STEAK AND MUSHROOM FILLING

3 FINISH AND BAKE THE PIE

1 MAKE THE QUICK PUFF PASTRY

1 Sift the flour and ½ tsp salt into a large bowl. Add one-third of the butter to the bowl and cut it into the flour with the round-bladed knives to form coarse crumbs.

2 Make a well in the center of the flour and butter mixture and pour the water into the well.

3 Draw in the flour and mix to a rough dough. If the dough is dry, add a little more water. Press the dough into a ball. Wrap it tightly and chill 15 minutes.

4 Roll out the dough on a lightly floured surface to a 6- x 15-inch rectangle. Cut the remaining butter into small pieces, then dot the pieces over two-thirds of the dough rectangle.

Dot butter over two-thirds of dough

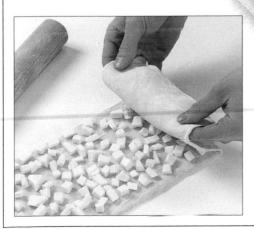

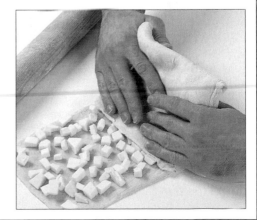

5 Fold the unbuttered dough over half of the buttered portion.

6 With both hands, fold the dough again so the butter pieces are completely enclosed in layers of dough.

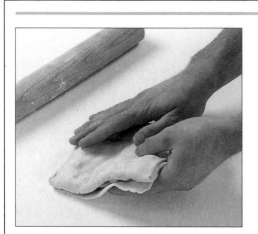

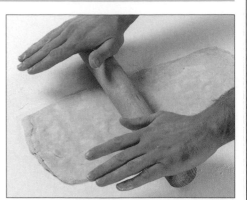

7 Turn the folded dough over and press the edges with the rolling pin to seal. Wrap and chill the dough 15 minutes.

8 Roll out the dough to a 6- x 18-inch rectangle, keeping the corners square.

! TAKE CARE !
Work quickly, rolling away from you and moving the dough on the floured surface so that it does not stick.

Butter will be distributed more evenly by each rolling

Lift dough with both hands to fold

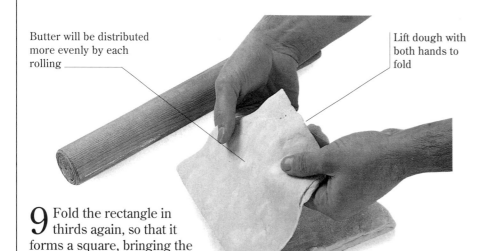

9 Fold the rectangle in thirds again, so that it forms a square, bringing the final fold toward you.

10 Turn the dough 90° so that the folded edge is to your left. Gently press the seams with the rolling pin to seal. This completes the first "turn." Repeat from step 8, to complete a second turn, then wrap the dough tightly and chill 15 minutes. Give the dough 2 more turns and chill again 15 minutes.

2 PREPARE THE STEAK AND MUSHROOM FILLING

Hold mushrooms stem-side down for slicing

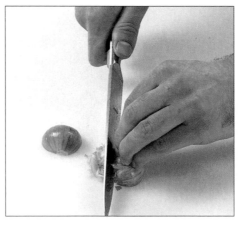

1 Heat the oven to 350° F. Wipe fresh mushrooms with damp paper towels and trim the stems. Cut them into medium slices. If using dried mushrooms, soak in a bowl of warm water until plump, about 30 minutes. Drain thoroughly and continue as for fresh mushrooms.

2 Peel the shallots, leaving a little of the root attached, and cut in half. Set each half flat-side down on the chopping board and slice horizontally toward the root, leaving the slices attached at the root. Slice vertically, again leaving the root end uncut, then cut across the shallot to make fine dice.

3 Strip the parsley leaves from the stems and pile the leaves on the chopping board. Holding a few of the leaves together with one hand, finely chop the leaves using the chef's knife.

4 Trim any fat and sinew from the beef chuck steak. Cut the meat into 1-inch cubes.

5 Season the flour with salt and pepper. Toss the steak in the flour to coat it, discarding the excess.

Coat meat cubes lightly and evenly with flour

6 Put the floured cubes of chuck steak in the casserole. Pour in the beef stock.

7 Add the sliced wild mushrooms and chopped shallots and stir well to mix. Bring to a boil on top of the stove, stirring the mixture constantly.

Crush meat against wooden spoon to test for tenderness

8 Cover the casserole and transfer to the heated oven. Cook, stirring occasionally, until the meat is tender enough to crush with your finger and the sauce is the consistency of light cream, 2-2¼ hours.

ANNE SAYS
"The meat should be almost covered with gravy. If necessary, add additional stock or water during cooking."

9 Stir in the chopped parsley and season to taste with salt and pepper. Spoon the pie filling into the pie dish with the funnel in the center. Let cool completely. Increase the oven heat to 425°F.

3 FINISH AND BAKE THE PIE

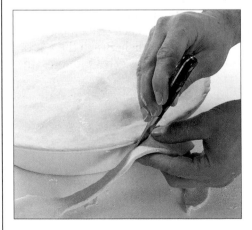

Roll out dough to even thickness

1 Lightly flour the work surface and roll out three-quarters of the chilled dough to a rough oval or circle at least 1 inch larger than the dish. Trim the edges and cut a strip the width of the dish rim from the edge of the dough.

2 Using the pastry brush, brush the flat rim of the pie dish with a little water, just to moisten.

3 Lay the strip of dough on the rim of the dish and press it down onto the rim. Lightly beat the egg with 1/2 tsp salt for the glaze. Brush the strip of dough with egg glaze.

ANNE SAYS
"*It's easier if you cut the strip of dough in half and then press on one piece of the dough at a time.*"

4 Roll the large piece of dough around the rolling pin and drape it over the pie.

! TAKE CARE !
Do not stretch the dough.

5 With your fingertips, press the dough firmly to seal it to the strip of dough on the rim of the pie dish.

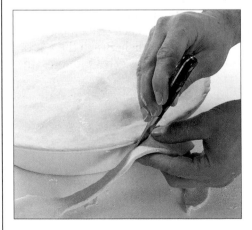

Egg glaze will give golden finish

Use tip of small knife to cut steam hole in dough lid

6 Trim off any excess dough with the small knife to make a neat finish.

7 Brush the top of the pie with the egg glaze. Cut a hole in the center of the dough lid, over the funnel, to allow steam to escape.

Use back of knife blade to mark leaf veins

8 Roll out the remaining dough and cut it into 1-inch strips. Cut across the dough strips diagonally to make leaf shapes. Mark veins on the leaves and curve them with your fingers.

9 Arrange the leaves on top of the pie and brush them with egg glaze. Chill the pie 15 minutes, then bake it in the heated oven until the top is golden brown, 25-35 minutes. If the top browns too quickly, cover it with foil.

⊗◎⊘ TO SERVE
Serve the pie hot from the dish. Cut the crust in wedges and scoop out the filling with a spoon.

Pastry has flaky, melt-in-the-mouth texture

INDIVIDUAL VICTORIAN STEAK AND KIDNEY PIES

In this hearty British favorite, kidneys and oysters are added to the steak instead of wild mushrooms.

1 Prepare the quick puff pastry as directed in the main recipe.
2 Peel off and discard the covering skin from 8 oz beef or lamb kidneys. Cut the ducts from the center of each kidney and cut into ½-inch cubes.
3 Prepare the shallots and parsley as directed; omit the mushrooms.
4 Prepare the beef chuck steak as directed and add 2 cups beef stock or water to the floured steak cubes in the casserole. Add the shallots and kidneys and cook as directed.
5 When the meat is very tender, stir in a dozen shucked medium oysters (about ½ pint) with their juice. Spoon the mixture into 4 individual casserole dishes and let cool completely.
6 Roll out the puff-pastry dough and cut out 4 rounds, each ½ inch bigger than a casserole dish. Brush the rim of each dish with egg glaze and top with the dough rounds, draping the dough over the edge of the dish and pressing it well over the rim to seal so it does not shrink during cooking.
7 Decorate the pies with dough flowers and crescents and bake as directed, allowing 20-25 minutes.

Wild mushrooms add depth of flavor to filling

HUNGARIAN BEEF GOULASH

🍽️ SERVES 4 🥣 WORK TIME 25-30 MINUTES ♨️ BAKING TIME 2½-3 HOURS

EQUIPMENT

chef's knife

kitchen scissors   small knife

wooden spoon

fork

2-pronged fork

small saucepan

bowls

2 teaspoons

aluminum foil

slotted spoon

casserole with lid

chopping board

Authentic goulash is half soup, half stew, made with beef and flavored with paprika, garlic, and bell peppers. True Hungarian paprika, aromatic and piquant, makes a great difference to this dish and can be found in Central European grocery stores. If it is not available, you may want to add more paprika to your taste with the onions.

GETTING AHEAD

The goulash can be made up to 2 days ahead and the flavor will mellow. Keep it, covered, in the refrigerator and reheat it on top of the stove.

SHOPPING LIST

6	medium onions, total weight about 1½ lb
2	garlic cloves
2 oz	smoked bacon
1 tbsp	vegetable oil
1½ lb	beef chuck steak
2 tbsp	paprika
½ tsp	caraway seeds
2 cups	water, more if needed
2	tomatoes
2	green bell peppers
	salt and pepper
½ cup	sour cream (optional)
	For the little dumplings
1	egg
6 tbsp	flour

INGREDIENTS

caraway seeds

beef chuck steak*

smoked bacon

sour cream (optional)

vegetable oil

flour

tomatoes

egg

garlic cloves

onions   paprika   green bell peppers

* skirt steak can also be used

ANNE SAYS
"Two types of paprika are commonly available. Hot paprika is piquant and robust, while mild paprika gives a mellow, sweeter flavor."

ORDER OF WORK

1 COOK THE GOULASH

2 FINISH THE GOULASH

3 PREPARE AND COOK THE DUMPLINGS

1 COOK THE GOULASH

Stir bacon so pieces brown evenly

1 Peel the onions, and cut in half. Slice each half horizontally, then vertically. Cut across to make dice. Set the flat side of the chef's knife on top of each garlic clove; strike it with your fist. Peel and finely chop the garlic.

2 Dice the bacon. Heat the oil in the casserole, add the bacon, and cook, stirring, until it is lightly browned and the bacon fat is rendered (melted down), 3-5 minutes. Stir in the onions.

3 Cut a piece of foil to fit inside the casserole, then cover the mixture and add the lid. Cook over low heat, stirring occasionally, until the onions are soft and translucent, 20-25 minutes. Do not let the onions burn.

4 Meanwhile, heat the oven to 350° F. Trim the beef chuck steak, discarding any fat. Cut the beef into 1½-inch strips, then across into 1½-inch cubes.

5 Stir the paprika into the onions and bacon and cook 2 minutes longer.

! TAKE CARE !
Do not let the paprika scorch.

Hungarian paprika has deep red color

6 Add the beef chuck steak, garlic, caraway seeds, and water to the casserole and stir to combine.

HOW TO CORE AND SEED A BELL PEPPER AND CUT IT INTO STRIPS OR DICE

The core and seeds of bell peppers must always be discarded.

1 With a small knife, cut around the pepper core and pull it out. Halve the pepper lengthwise and scrape out the seeds. Cut away the white ribs on the inside.

2 Set each pepper half cut-side down on the work surface and press down with the heel of your hand to flatten it.

3 With a chef's knife, slice the pepper half lengthwise into strips. For dice, gather the strips together in a pile and cut across into squares.

7 Bring to a boil, stirring well, then cover with the lid and transfer to the heated oven. Cook until the beef is almost tender when pierced with the 2-pronged fork, 1-1½ hours. Stir occasionally, adding more water if the onions start to stick.

Heat goulash to boiling on top of stove before transferring to oven

FINISH THE GOULASH

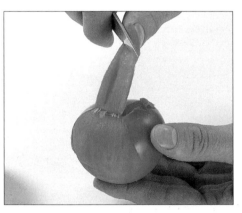

1 Cut the cores from the tomatoes and score an "x" on the base of each with the tip of a knife. Immerse them in a pan of boiling water until the skin starts to split, 8-15 seconds. Using the slotted spoon, transfer the tomatoes at once to a bowl of cold water. When cold, peel off the skin. Cut the tomatoes crosswise in half and squeeze out the seeds; chop each half.

2 Core and seed the green bell peppers and cut them into strips (see box, left). Stir the green peppers and tomatoes into the goulash. Season to taste with salt and pepper.

3 Cover and continue cooking until the meat is very soft, 30-45 minutes longer. Taste the stew for seasoning; it should be rich and thick.

3 PREPARE AND COOK THE DUMPLINGS

1 Lightly beat the egg in a small bowl. Put the flour and a pinch of salt in another small bowl; stir in the egg.

! TAKE CARE !
Do not overmix to an elastic consistency because this makes the dumplings tough.

Take care to mix batter gently

Do not overmix batter and make it elastic like this

2 Transfer the goulash to the top of the stove and heat to boiling. Using the 2 teaspoons, drop spoonfuls of the dumpling mixture into the goulash and simmer until cooked through, 5-7 minutes.

🍴 **TO SERVE**
Ladle the goulash and dumplings into individual warmed soup bowls and top each serving with a spoonful of sour cream, if you like.

Little dumplings are simmered on top of succulent stew just before serving

HUNGARIAN VEAL GOULASH

Cubes of veal are the basis for this goulash, with potatoes added for body.

1 Substitute 1½ lb lean boneless stewing veal for the beef and cook it with the onions, garlic, and caraway seeds as directed.

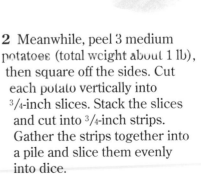

2 Meanwhile, peel 3 medium potatoes (total weight about 1 lb), then square off the sides. Cut each potato vertically into ¾-inch slices. Stack the slices and cut into ¾-inch strips. Gather the strips together into a pile and slice them evenly into dice.

3 Add the potatoes to the casserole with the green bell peppers and tomatoes. Continue cooking until they are tender and the meat is very soft, 45-60 minutes. Omit the dumplings.

MEAT KNOW-HOW

What we call meat is muscle tissue. The harder the muscle works, the tougher it is. Tender meat comes from young animals, or from the less active parts of older animals, such as the hindquarters, the loin, and particularly the tenderloin or fillet (which is protected by the ribs and hardly moves at all). However, youth or inactivity are not in themselves decisive indicators of quality – immature meat can be bland, while the tenderloin and other inactive muscles tend to have less flavor than tougher meat.

CHOOSING AND SERVING

There are a few general rules for selecting all meat. Look for good butchering (a skilled meat cutter follows the contours of muscle and bone), with small cuts sliced evenly or in uniform pieces so that they will cook at the same speed. Cuts should be trimmed of sinew, leaving just enough fat to keep the flesh moist. Marbling is the key to the flavor and

tenderness of meat. Veal and baby lamb have little marbling, but older lamb or mutton, and to a lesser extent pork, should be lightly streaked with fat. With beef, marbling is a clear indication of quality.

Meat should have a clear but not bright color: a grayish tinge is a bad sign. Yellow fat signals old age (except in beef from certain breeds, such as British Jersey and Guernsey cattle), and dried edges betray dehydration in meat.

Servings for meat depend on the type of meat and the cut you are preparing. As a rough guide, for 1 person you should allow $1/2$ pound of boneless meat or $3/4$ to 1 pound of meat on the bone.

STORING MEAT

At home, meat should be stored, loosely wrapped in plastic, in the coldest part of the refrigerator. Variety meats, ground meat, and cuts such as veal scaloppine are best eaten within 1 day; chops, steaks, and small pieces can be kept for 2-3 days; large roasts will remain in good condition for up to 5 days. Red meats keep better than white meats, and lean cuts better than fatty ones, because fat turns rancid before meat starts to spoil.

An unpleasant smell, slimy surface, and greenish tinge are all danger signs that meat has been stored at too high a temperature or for too long and that bacteria have developed. Problems caused by rapid commercial chilling of the carcass, which toughens fibers, are less easily detected, although pallid color and a wet package are an indication.

MEAT AND YOUR HEALTH

Meat, especially beef, has been criticized for its high saturated fat content. Prime, the highest grade of beef, is the one containing the most fat. This has led to the development of leaner "light" meat with up to 25 percent less fat than the standard product. Cooking techniques that don't add more fat to the dish, such as simmering, roasting, and broiling, are another healthy option. These can be found in French Hot Pot, Roast Leg of Lamb, and Turkish Ground Lamb Kebabs. And it's easy to make other meat dishes more healthy without losing significant flavor. First of all, cut down on the amount of meat per portion and increase the vegetables; this reduces the calories, too. Trim off all excess fat from the meat you use. Omit rich accompaniments, such as the Marsala sauce from Veal Piccate – serve the scaloppine with the pan juices deglazed with a little white wine. Omit the bacon, lean salt pork, and kneaded butter from Provençal Beef Stew, and use a little arrowroot to thicken the sauce. When frying and sautéing, butter can be replaced with olive or vegetable oil, or with polyunsaturated margarine. However, pastry recipes will suffer in taste and texture without some butter content. Make these small changes and your favorite meat recipes will be better for your health and still taste great.

FREEZING

Frozen meat varies in quality depending on how quickly it is frozen and how much fat it contains. Because quick freezing causes less damage to the texture and juiciness of meat, smaller pieces freeze more successfully than large cuts. Fat gradually turns rancid, even in the coldest temperatures, so a lean piece of beef will keep better than a well-marbled rib roast. Careful wrapping is vital, not only to prevent freezer burn, but also because exposure to oxygen accelerates spoilage. Beef and lamb can be frozen up to 1 year, depending on the cuts, while veal and pork lose quality rapidly after 8 months.

For convenience, meat is best frozen ready to use as individual chops, chunks for stew, or patties of ground meat. However, very thin slices of meat tend to dry out, so they should be cut after thawing. Stews and cooked meats in sauce freeze well, but plain roasts and sliced cooked meats tend to dry out, even when securely wrapped.

THAWING

Frozen meat is usually thawed loosely wrapped in the refrigerator. Large cuts may need up to 5 hours per pound. Thawing completely before cooking helps retain the juiciness in meat, but if you must cook an unthawed piece of meat in an emergency, allow one and a half times the cooking time. Meat can also be thawed in the microwave or by immersing it, tightly wrapped, in a bowl of warm water.

! TAKE CARE !

Never refreeze raw meat. Frozen meat should be cooked within 12 hours of thawing, especially meat stored with gravy.

MICROWAVE

Meat cooked in the microwave oven is often juicier than meat prepared in a conventional oven, and obviously it cooks much more quickly. The microwave will cook stews and meats in gravy to perfection; it also is good for reheating, allowing the flavor to mellow without overcooking. Keep in mind that a microwave oven works best with tougher cuts; more tender meat tends to dry out during cooking so it is preferable to roast or broil these cuts in a conventional oven or to grill on a barbecue. Defrosting meat is one of the great uses of a microwave, particularly for large cuts, but take care: some meats may thaw unevenly.

HOW-TO BOXES

There are pictures of all preparation steps for each **Meat Classics** *recipe. Some basic techniques are used in a number of recipes; they are shown in extra detail in these special "how-to" boxes.*

DECORATIONS FOR MEAT

The presentation of a meat dish improves dramatically with a colorful decoration.
I find that fresh vegetables are often the most eye-catching. Here are just a few ideas.

HOMEMADE POTATO CHIPS

Homemade potato chips are an easy, delicious accompaniment for grilled meats, particularly steak.

1 Peel large firm potatoes (1/2-1 per person). Slice each potato paper-thin using the slicing blade of a grater. Alternatively, you can use a mandoline or the thin slicing blade of a food processor. Rinse the potato slices and pat them dry.

2 Heat vegetable oil in a deep-fat fryer to 375° F. Fry the potato slices, in batches if necessary, for 2-3 minutes until dark golden and crisp. Drain on paper towels.

3 Sprinkle the chips with salt and serve.

WATERCRESS BOUQUETS

Small or large bouquets of watercress make an attractive decoration for roasted or broiled meats.

1 Divide the sprigs of a bunch of watercress, then wash and dry them thoroughly. Align a small bunch firmly in one hand. Twist with the other hand to snap off the stems and discard them.

2 Drop the leaves, stems down, onto the plate to form an attractive bouquet. Alternatively, for a large roast, use the whole bunch to form a giant bouquet.

SHOESTRING VEGETABLES

Shoestring vegetables resemble colorful spaghetti, good with meats in sauce.

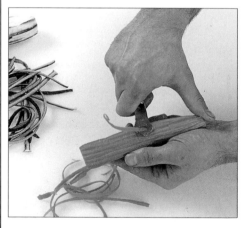

1 If using carrots, peel them. For zucchini, use only the colored skin. With a citrus stripper or channeling knife, take fine shoestring-like strips lengthwise from the vegetable.

2 Blanch the vegetable shoestrings in boiling salted water until just tender, about 1 minute. Drain well and add salt and pepper.

3 If liked, toss with a little melted butter, then arrange on each warmed plate in a small, neat pile.

RIBBON VEGETABLES

Thin ribbons of vegetables such as carrot, zucchini, daikon, and parsnip make attractive decorations, particularly if you mix different colors.

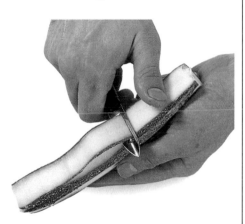

1 Peel or trim the vegetable, then cut off thin shavings lengthwise using a vegetable peeler.

2 Blanch the vegetable ribbons in boiling salted water until just tender, 1-2 minutes. Drain well and sprinkle with chopped parsley or other fresh herbs, salt, and pepper.

3 Toss the vegetable ribbons with the herbs and seasoning, then arrange on each warmed plate in a small, neat pile.

TOMATO ROSES

Roses of spiraled tomato peel are a colorful and decorative addition to any plate.

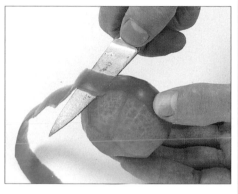

1 Using a small sharp knife, peel the skin from a firm, medium, or large tomato, starting at the flower end opposite the core and peeling the skin in a long continuous strip.

2 Holding the flower end of the strip of peel between the thumb and forefinger of one hand and guiding the rest of the peel with the fingers of your other hand, turn the flower end to form a spiral or rose; hold it in place with your thumb.

3 Tuck in the end of the strip and set the rose on the plate to be decorated.

CARROT OR GREEN BEAN BUNDLES

Carrots, cut into matchsticks, or fine green beans tied with a strip of zucchini skin make elegant garnishes for meat dishes, particularly those with a sauce.

1 If using green beans, trim them to 2½-inch lengths. For carrots, peel them and cut into fine matchstick strips 2½ inches long. Cook the beans or carrot strips in boiling salted water until tender.

2 Meanwhile, thinly peel a strip of skin from a zucchini with a vegetable peeler and cut it into fine "strings" using a chef's knife. Blanch in boiling salted water until pliable, about 1 minute; drain well.

3 Drain the beans or carrots. Arrange them in small bundles and tie each bundle with a string of zucchini. Finish with a neat twist or bow.

INDEX

ACKNOWLEDGMENTS

Photographers David Murray
Jules Selmes
Assisted by Ian Boddy

Chef Eric Treuille
Cookery Consultant Linda Collister
Assisted by Joanna Pitchfork

US Editor Jeanette Mall

Typesetting Rowena Feeny
Assisted by Robert Moore
Text film by Disc to Print (UK) Limited

Production Consultant Lorraine Baird

*Anne Willan would like to thank
her chief editor Cynthia Nims and
associate editor Kate Krader for their
vital help with writing the book and
researching and testing the recipes,
aided by La Varenne's chefs
and trainees.*

WEIGHTS AND MEASURES

MEASUREMENT CONVERSIONS

US Cups	Metric
1 tbsp	15 mL
$\frac{1}{8}$ cup	30 mL
$\frac{1}{4}$ cup	60 mL
$\frac{3}{8}$ cup	90 mL
$\frac{1}{2}$ cup	125 mL
$\frac{2}{3}$ cup	150 mL
$\frac{3}{4}$ cup	175 mL
1 cup ($\frac{1}{2}$ pint)	250 mL
1 $\frac{1}{4}$ cups	300 mL
1 $\frac{1}{2}$ cups	375 mL
2 cups (1 pint)	500 mL
2 $\frac{1}{2}$ cups	600 mL
3 $\frac{3}{4}$ cups	900 mL
1 qt (4 cups)	1 litre
1 $\frac{1}{4}$ quarts	1.25 litres
3 US pints	1.5 litres
2 litres	2 quarts

Standards

1 tsp = 5 mL
1 tbsp =15 mL
1 fl oz = 30 mL
1 mL = 0.035 fl oz
1 UK pint = 20 fl oz
1 US pint = 16 fl oz
1 litre = 33 fl oz
    (1 US qt)

Length Conversions

1 cm = 0.3 in

SOLID WEIGHT CONVERSIONS

US	Metric
$\frac{1}{2}$ oz	15 g
1 oz	30 g
2 oz	60g
3 oz	90g
4 oz ($\frac{1}{4}$ lb)	120 g
5 oz	150 g
6 oz	180g
8 oz ($\frac{1}{2}$ lb)	240 g
12 oz ($\frac{3}{4}$ lb)	360 g
1 lb (16 oz)	480 g

Standards

1 oz = 30 g	1 lb = 16 oz (480 g)
1 g – 0.35 oz	1 kg = 2.2 lb

OVEN TEMPERATURE CONVERSIONS

°F	Gas	°C
225	$\frac{1}{4}$	110
250	$\frac{1}{2}$	120
275	1	140
300	2	150
325	3	160
350	4	175
375	5	190
400	6	200
425	7	220
450	8	230
475	9	240
500	10	260